Original Design

Set Free to be Who God Created

DENISE BUSS

CloverFields
Publishing

TRUTH ♣ DELIVERANCE ♣ FREEDOM

Cl♣verFields
Publishing
P.O. Box 2113, Maple Grove, MN 55311
Denise@cloverfieldspublishing.com

www.CloverFieldsPublishing.com

Printed in the United States of America
Editor: Heidi Sheard
Cover and interior design: Purpose Design

Unless otherwise noted, Scripture quotations are taken from the New King James Version®. Copyright © 1982 by Thomas Nelson, Inc. Used by permission. All rights reserved.
Scripture quotations marked MES are taken from The Message. Copyright © 1993, 1994, 1995, 1996, 2000, 2001, 2002. Used by permission of NavPress Publishing Group.

Publishers Cataloging In Publication
Buss, Denise.
Original Design: set free to be who God created / Denise Buss.—1st ed.
    p. cm.
ISBN 978-0-9903583-7-4 (softcover)
ISBN 978-0-9903583-3-6 (IE)
1. Christianity. 2. Freedom in Christ. 3. Spiritual authority. 4. Deliverance. I. Title.

Library of Congress Control Number: 2015908842

I dedicate this book to my heavenly Father,
my Savior Jesus, and the Holy Spirit who
guides me into all truth.
And to all those who are poor in spirit,
brokenhearted, captive, blind, and oppressed.

Acknowledgments

I WOULD LIKE TO GIVE SPECIAL THANKS to Ed Caton. If not for his obedience to God and his devoted friendship I would have a very different story to tell. He has helped me spiritually, emotionally, and financially, and I am forever grateful. You are my most cherished friend.

Hannah Mae, I thank you for the many times you sacrificed our time together so I could be obedient to God. You are truly my precious gift from above.

I want to thank my mom for believing in me even when she doesn't understand my decisions. I appreciate your love, kindness, and generosity to Hannah and me.

Thank you, Kristi and Dick Strassburg, for your endearing friendship, prayers, and financial help.

Contents

Dedication iii

Acknowledgments. v

Foreword ix

Introduction xi

The Journey

1 The Crisis 1

2 Set up for Destruction. 5

3 Validation. 13

4 God's Invitation 17

5 The Subtle Pulling Away. 25

6 The Wake-up Call 31

7 Who is My Father?. 37

8 Authority in Christ. 61

9 Killing the Old Man 79

10 Fear Not 103

11 Butter Melts. 125

12 Leaving the Station. 149

13 The Great Physician 167

14 Casting Crowns 185

15 New Territory 209

Appendices

A Steps to Salvation. 227

B Baptism in the Holy Spirit 233

C Authority and Power of God 239

Foreword

MORE AND MORE PEOPLE are being hit with depression, fear, and anxiety. Mind-altering drugs and sleeping pills have become regular items in many medicine cabinets. People are searching for the peace that eludes them. Denise Buss was no exception. She became paralyzed by fear and anxiety and couldn't see a way out. As Denise's story unfolds in the pages of this book, you will find encouragement that you are not alone. And even more importantly, you will see that there is a way out of the oppression that torments you or someone you love.

When Denise cried out to God for help, her heavenly Father sent someone to bring about God's plan for her life. Her courage and obedience to God broke the demonic hold that Satan had on her. Denise's most important realization was that it wasn't just one incident that put her in this pit of agony, but layers and layers of wrong thinking and abuse. Therefore, it was going to take not just a renewal of her mind, but also deliverance and inner healing. Forgiving wrongs that had been done to her was an important step to her spiritual freedom. Because Denise was willing to make the effort and be persistent, her life was transformed into His Original Design—the glorious creation

God had always intended it to be. You may not have a friend like she did to walk you out of your imprisonment, but we all have the precious Holy Spirit, the Helper, to guide us into freedom.

Original Design is a treasure chest of personal stories, valuable examples, and the most relevant Scriptures. If you are seeking the peace and happiness that our Father intended for us to enjoy, Denise's experience, as told in this book, will give you a boldness to put on the Armor of God and fight against the enemy who works to destroy us all.

—**Peggy Joyce Ruth**, author of *Tormented, Eight Years and Back, Trust the Lord and You will not be Disappointed,* and several books for various ages titled, *Psalm 91: God's Shield of Protection.*

Introduction

WE ARE HURTING, BROKEN PEOPLE—whether our wounds are visible to us or not. Having been bruised by life in one way or another, we need the Great Physician to heal us—body and soul. This requires dealing with matters of the heart; personal, painful matters that if left unattended will cost us in our relationships with others and more importantly with God.

This is not a story about a tragic childhood. It's not just another book on transformation. This book shows that there are spiritual consequences to the common events and choices in our lives. You'll see how Satan used my life experiences to distort my beliefs about God and myself. Satan's ultimate plan was to destroy me, but if he couldn't succeed, then at least he would prevent me from becoming who God created me to be and doing what God intended me to do. The power of God is bigger than any scheme of the devil!

Original Design is primarily derived from nearly eighty prayer sessions with my pastor friend, Ed, spanning over a period of three years. Ed and I quickly realized that the Holy Spirit was actively speaking and working during these intense prayer times, so we recorded each session to preserve the accuracy of His great work.

Initially, prayer meetings were held because the devil was jeopardizing my life in a specific way. I usually came to God in great distress; filled with fear or despair, and desperate to hear from Him. God not only used our prayer sessions to rescue me from the attacks of the enemy, but He also revealed secrets and unburied lies hidden deep in my heart. Once God exposed and removed them, He replaced them with His truths. As time went on, I changed from a helpless girl cowering in the corner to a mighty soldier in God's army; from seeing myself as a worthless, unwanted burden to a favored daughter of the King. As the Holy Spirit intimately embraced my heart and mind, I was set free from the works of Satan and my wounds were healed.

Each prayer time had at least one gift of the Spirit in operation. The gifts of the Holy Spirit are listed in 1 Corinthians 12:7-11. "But the manifestation of the Spirit is given to each one for the profit of *all*: for to one is given the word of wisdom through the Spirit, to another the word of knowledge through the same Spirit, to another faith by the same Spirit, to another gifts of healings by the same Spirit, to another the working of miracles, to another prophecy, to another discerning of spirits, to another *different* kinds of tongues, to another the interpretation of tongues. But one and the same Spirit works all these things, distributing to each one individually as He wills."

The subject of tongues is found many places in the New Testament and the Apostle Paul spent the better portion of forty verses in 1 Corinthians 14 discussing the topic of tongues, including interpretation, and also prophecy. Paul said when we pray in tongues we do not speak to men, but to God and we edify ourselves in the process (1 Cor. 14:2-4). Paul wanted all the believers in the Corinthian church to speak with tongues (1 Cor. 14:5), so we can assume he desired this for all believers everywhere.

I believe the gift of tongues listed in 1 Corinthians 12:10 is different from the tongues Paul often talked about—the tongues we receive when we are baptized in the Holy Spirit. The former can be given to a believer by the Holy Spirit anytime He wants. Since it's given as the Holy Spirit wills, a person may only be able to speak in tongues once and never again. In contrast, when a believer is baptized in the Holy Spirit, the ability to speak in tongues is indefinite (see appendix C). This is the type of tongues that Ed and I have, and it was used to some degree in almost all of our prayer sessions. We prayed in tongues to strengthen our spirits and this helped us to be more tuned in to the Holy Spirit within us.

Most of the time interpretation wasn't needed. First Corinthians 14:2 says, "For he who speaks in a tongue does not speak to men but to God, for no one understands him; however, in the spirit he speaks mysteries." Tongues, when used in our personal prayer time, does not need to be understood by us or anyone else to be effective. Even so, God gave Ed the gift of interpreting my tongues on a few special occasions.

Most of the information I received from God came through Ed in the form of words of knowledge. This knowledge originated in God, and Ed was but a conduit for these supernatural, God-imparted words. Without these God-given disclosures, Ed could not have helped me. These insights not only gave us strategies during spiritual warfare, but also unlocked the secrets and mysteries of my past so they could no longer be hindrances to my deliverance and healing. Often times having information wasn't enough. In those situations, God gave Ed a word of wisdom so we could apply the knowledge He'd given us.

A few times, Ed also received the gift of prophecy. This gift entails receiving a message from God and having an anointed utterance to communicate it. Prophecy usually involves foretelling future events, but it can sometimes simply refer to declaring God's will. It is always done under revelation or inspiration from the Holy Spirit.

There were instances when both Ed and I were given the gift of discerning spirits. This gift gives insight into the supernatural realm and can be helpful in a few different ways. There were occasions when the Holy Spirit gave Ed the ability to discern my heart, thoughts, or feelings. Other times, when either of us received this gift, we were able to perceive evil spirits in or on people, on objects, or in the environment around us.

Acts 2:17 says, "And it shall come to pass in the last days, says God, that I will pour out of My Spirit on all flesh; your sons and your daughters shall prophesy, your young men shall see visions, your old men shall dream dreams." Both Ed and I had visions during our prayer time and we each had several God-given dreams. Many times we didn't know what the dreams meant until God gave Ed a word of knowledge to explain them.

The gifts of the Holy Spirit are our supernatural God manifesting Himself through His people. They ought to be a regular occurrence throughout our walk with God and should not be viewed as unusual or only for those "crazy charismatics." I ask you to keep an open heart and mind as I share my story with you. Let the Holy Spirit bear witness with your spirit that His gifts are available to help set you free!

And you shall know the truth,
and the truth shall make you free.
—John 8:32

The Crisis

The thief does not come except to steal, and to kill, and to destroy.
—John 10:10

IT'S MY FINAL NIGHT in the second-floor guest room of my parents' apartment complex. My death is imminent. While my four-year-old daughter sleeps just a few feet away, I'm in hand-to-hand combat with the devil himself.

I had recently started taking sleeping pills so I could function in my job. I was afraid to take the medication when I was alone with my daughter, so in the evenings we went to my parents' apartment to sleep. This was my only option for relief to my situation. I didn't want anyone to know how much I was struggling, and I knew my parents wouldn't ask questions. After sleeping there a couple of nights, the manager informed my mom that their policy forbids overnight guests. Since management had this rule, they kept rooms available on the second floor for visitors to use on a short-term basis. My mother offered to rent us one for a few nights, and I accepted. The guest room was simple, just one room with a double bed and a bathroom. I didn't sleep any better here, but I did have a sense of security with my parents in the building in case I needed them for support.

It's now our third night in the guest room and the devil escalates his attack. As I pace the floor between the bed and the bathroom, he spews words of death and destruction at me. He pounds my mind with thoughts that God has not forgiven me for neglecting Him and has turned His back on me.

I believe Satan's lies that I'm rejected, and I'm horrified at the thought of a future without God. I'm filled with terror as the Evil One torments me with visions of Hell. I see myself crying in agony, gnashing my teeth. Worms eating away at my flesh. It's a picture of everlasting darkness and suffering for all eternity—with no hope of escape.

In an attempt to fight the growing darkness and fear, I quote prayers from a scripture confession book. As I speak the prayers, my heart pounds and the knot in my stomach tightens so much so that I can barely walk. I do my best to cling to God's Word; professing that I'm inseparable from God's love and that with God, I can stand against Satan.

The devil is not deterred by my feeble attempt to resist him and his lies. I cannot see him, but I sense him walking alongside of me laughing. I can almost feel his breath on my face as he ridicules, "You don't even believe what you're saying. Besides, prayer won't help. God has already cast you out. It's too late for you."

The clock on the bedside table reads 1:00 a.m. Exhausted, I lie down in bed, hoping to get some rest. As soon as I pull the blanket up to my chin, I'm overwhelmed with an impulse to run out the door and fling myself over the balcony. The fall to the foyer floor would surely kill me, I thought.

I look at my daughter sleeping peacefully and imagine her reaction when she sees my body splattered on the tile in a pool of blood. This powerful impulse toward suicide is not mine. Who in their right mind would think such thoughts! Still, the voices urging me to kill myself are undeniably strong. All I can do is cry out to God for strength and beg Him to have mercy on me.

By the grace of God, I make it through the night. When my daughter awakens, I help her get dressed and take her downstairs to have breakfast with my parents. Without a word, I return to our room and sit on the edge of the bed. The accusations continue with a vengeance.

With my narrow escape from suicide the night before, I realize I can no longer fight the devil on my own. I am mentally and physically exhausted from weeks of high anxiety affecting my ability to eat and sleep properly, and I'm spiritually weak with no defenses. I've done all I know to do. It's not enough. Something has to change.

The past two years had been a rough season with the demands of work and family life and I had been neglecting my time with God. I was employed as a nurse practitioner, caring for people with liver disease. I enjoyed the job itself, but in addition to an eight-hour work day, I spent two hours in the car commuting. On the way home each day, I picked up my daughter and then rushed to make dinner and salvage what was left of the evening. Most nights and weekends were spent at gymnastics or soccer and trying to manage life as a single mom. During this period of time, my relationship with God became lukewarm at best.

I was estranged from God until recently, when He opened my eyes to my half-heartedness and showed me the painful truth that I was no longer sensitive to the Holy Spirit. I cried out to Him for forgiveness and asked Him back into my life. As I read the Bible, it came alive to me again and brought life and encouragement to my soul. Though I was tired, I started praying in the evenings and God blessed me with renewed energy, joy, and devotion to Him.

This fresh allegiance enraged Satan. He began to engage me in a series of mental skirmishes to thwart my renewed commitment to God. He scattered seeds of doubt about God's love for me and my salvation. After a few weeks, Satan's lies became like weeds tangled in my heart, and anxiety and sleeplessness flourished. Now struggling in this guest room, where can I turn for help?

I decide to call my pastor friend Ed and tell him I am in a crisis. He offers to meet me at my house at noon to pray. I phone my sister and tell her I'm having some emotional problems and that I need her to come get my daughter Hannah and care for her until I can work through my issues. She's confused by this, but knows by the sound of my voice not to ask questions.

I go downstairs to my parents' apartment to tell my mom that Dawn is coming to pick up Hannah. Thankfully, my parents had the sense not to say much. They just let me say my goodbye to my daughter. I lean down and whisper, "I love you."

"I love you too," Hannah says, just as she always did. Her bottom lip quivers and her arms stretch toward me for a hug. She knows something's wrong with her mama. Surely she must realize that I might never come back for her. I wrap my arms around my precious girl and reassure her, "Auntie Dawn will take good care of you. And I will see you soon." I leave in tears.

It is my darkest hour. I'm no longer capable of caring for my daughter, or even for myself. I don't know if I'm going to live or die, be sentenced to Heaven or Hell. I don't even know if I'll be able to function well enough to be a mom again.

Set up for Destruction

No weapon formed against you shall prosper,
and every tongue which rises against you in judgment You shall condemn.
—Isaiah 54:17

I GREW UP IN A HOME where God was acknowledged, but not obeyed or invited into our daily lives. Without God's guidance, my parents couldn't help but follow Satan's leadings, and he used them to spawn a distorted self-image in me. This was the foundation on which Satan built his plan of destruction for my life.

My dad was the youngest of six children and the son of an alcoholic who physically and verbally abused his mother. After serving in the Navy during World War II, he felt compelled to move back in with his parents to protect his mother from his father's abuse. He stayed there until the age of twenty-six when she died. He had two failed marriages before he met my mother. She became his third wife and the only one with whom he had children.

My dad rarely talked to me or looked at me. He certainly never showed me any affection. I wasn't allowed to sit on his lap or give him hugs and kisses. He frequently degraded me and called me names such as *dumb* and *stupid*. He criticized me for the Bs on my report cards, once scolding me so much that I ran into my bedroom and hid in the closet and cried.

One night when I was seven, as I lay in bed, I looked down the hall into the bathroom and saw him shaving. When he noticed me watching him, he shot me a look of disgust and slammed the door. I felt worthless.

Dad continued to reject me throughout my childhood, seeing me as nothing more than a bothersome obligation. I often heard him complain to my mom that his children cost him too much money. My mom tried to explain my dad's behavior by telling us that he never wanted children. Her painful words only sealed the message in my heart; I was an unwanted burden.

Despite my dad's disapproval, I tried hard to please him. I did my best to be quiet, do my chores, and get good grades. In spite of all my efforts, I never received the love from him I was seeking.

My mom met my physical needs, but wasn't capable of satisfying my emotional needs—past hurts had caused her to close her own heart. My mom was born out of wedlock and considered an illegitimate child. Her mother forced her to lie about who her father was and to spy on her real dad and give her reports about his behavior. At the age of seven, Mom was sexually molested by a male relative. She never told a soul. When she was seventeen, she married an alcoholic who basically left her on her own to raise their two young children.

When my dad came into her life, he promised to take care of her and her kids. But shortly after their marriage, two more unwanted children came. He stayed away from home as much as possible. When he was home, he was cold-hearted and verbally abusive.

Despite her broken and scarred heart, my mom tried to love me. We baked cookies during the holidays, she went to my school programs, and we worked puzzles together. But we had no intimacy. I couldn't share with her my fears or problems, nor my dreams or aspirations.

As I grew up, my mom's attempts to educate me about life were shallow at best. We didn't discuss the importance of kindness, patience, or other worthwhile virtues. She didn't teach me about sex or the possibility of chastity.

My mom could not meet my need for love or acceptance; she was unable to give me what she didn't have. She raised me the same way her mother had raised her. She expected me to hide problems and bury secrets. It was acceptable to lie to protect myself and others. I accepted her warped philosophies and then used them to justify my behavior.

My siblings were also used to shape my self-image. My half-brother, who is eight years older, served as my surrogate father. He took me hunting, played video games with me, and wrestled with me in the living room. At the local carnival, he carried me on his shoulders and we went on rides together. One year he tried so hard to win me a stuffed animal. He ended up buying the biggest one they had because he knew it would make me happy. I'll never forget that night. I was smiling from ear to ear!

I loved my half-brother and I knew I could trust him. That's why my heart broke when he unexpectedly left home to live with his biological father. At the age of eight, I lost my only source of love and comfort. I was devastated by the sudden emptiness.

Love and approval from my older sister was now even more important to me. Unfortunately, she was unaware of my emotional needs and frequently voiced her opinions of me, both good and bad.

Her words of disapproval cut deep, so I tried to change to gain her acceptance. This caused me to develop a life-long habit of looking to my sister for my identity and seeking her approval.

I saw myself as an unwanted nuisance who wasn't worthy of love or deserving of any good thing. Satan had me right where he wanted me.

My understanding of self was defined by my dad's rejection, my mom's neglect, my brother's abandonment, and my sister's appraisals. I saw myself as an unwanted nuisance who wasn't worthy of love or deserving of any good thing. Satan had me right where he wanted me.

In Genesis 1:26, God said, "Let Us make man in Our image, according to Our likeness." I was created in the image and likeness of God. If only I'd have known. . .

In addition to my family, Satan used my upbringing in a small, rural church to negatively influence my self-portrait. My church taught me that God was mean, angry, and to be feared—just like my dad. They told me I was full of sin, which was true. But rather than teaching me how to be forgiven, they made me feel guilty about my sins. This reinforced what I already believed: I was unacceptable.

Our church required everyone to go to God through a priest they called "father." I knelt at the confessional and declared my sins and guilt to him through a small screen in a door. This proved to me that I wasn't worthy of approaching God myself.

Then again, why would I want to talk to a God who was as impersonal as my dad and the father at church? Besides, God wouldn't approve of me either. As bad as I was, I would never get into Heaven. My only hope was purgatory. This depiction of God's character caused me to run and hide from Him. When I left my parents' home at seventeen, I stopped going to church. I didn't return for many years.

Satan also transformed my character to be more like his and turned me away from God and the life He intended for me by using our culture. He influenced me through television, music, and spiritual "entertainment."

As a child I watched horror films with my family. These movies planted terrifying images in my mind and horrific fears in my heart. For example, I dreaded having to get the mail. The mailbox was about a hundred feet from our house. In winter, when darkness came early, I made my mother watch out the window while I ran as fast as I could to the mailbox. My heart pounded and my eyes darted to and fro as I looked for someone or something waiting to grab me. Every time I made it back, I was grateful my life had been spared.

Our family had a lake home, and I learned to water-ski at a young age. When I fell down and had to wait for the boat to circle back around to get me, I panicked, afraid I might find a dead body floating nearby. As I frantically looked in the water, I kept my body still and close to the surface, hoping to keep from becoming entangled with a corpse that might be lurking just beneath me.

Our basement was another source of fear. It had a storage room with splatters of red paint on one of the walls. To me it looked like the "red room" from a movie called *The Amityville Horror*. Every time

I had to go in there, bloody scenes flooded my mind. I also avoided the garage; it was filled with sharp, menacing tools. In recurring nightmares, I was either cut up with the hedge trimmer or beaten to death with a hammer.

Satan had used movies as a mechanism to immerse me in fear and exert demonic influence in my life. They were realistic to my young and naïve heart; I felt certain those things would happen to me and I would die a violent death. I didn't speak of these fears, so I had no one to comfort me. I never felt safe.

When I got older and wiser, I stopped watching these movies, and instead chose films that emphasized money and romance. I believed that if I accumulated enough expensive clothes and flashy jewelry, I would be like the glamorous women the movies portrayed. I bought the lie that I could buy happiness. I thought this was my ticket to being important and valuable, or at least respected.

I became selfish and greedy, and I valued my belongings above all else. I used brand-name clothes, designer watches, and gold jewelry to project an image of who I wanted to be. But no matter how much stuff I had or how attractive I looked on the outside, I was still ugly ole me on the inside.

These movie characters I admired were involved in romantic affairs with handsome men who were successful and wealthy. When they won over the man's heart, they were often rescued from a life of despair. For many years I tried to accomplish the same; I gave my body to men in hopes they might whisk me away from my problems. That never happened.

Satan also swayed me with music. Whenever I felt disheartened, I found sympathy in the lyrics, which enabled me to justify my feelings. The songs often suggested I'd feel better if I drank alcohol or found a new boyfriend. Music also beckoned me to the dance floor. When I danced my inhibitions were swept away by the intoxicating rhythm and I expressed myself in ways that would make a sailor blush. In reality this ungodly music stimulated pity parties, fed selfishness, and aroused negative ideas. Everything it encouraged led me deeper into sin and further away from God.

The most clever and yet elusive ploy Satan used against me was spiritual "entertainment." The concept of "harmless magic" was engrained in me at an early age. Santa magically came down the chimney, and the tooth fairy mysteriously exchanged money for my teeth. There were magic spells, a genie in a magic lamp who granted wishes, and magic carpet rides—to name a few. The enchantments continued with Harry Potter, an adolescent wizard who attends a school of witchcraft and wizardry. With a keen interest in the supernatural, my sister and I started playing with a Ouija board. We tried to make spirits answer our questions. They didn't respond, so I assumed they weren't listening, or they didn't want to talk. Maybe they weren't even real.

I once saw a movie with voodoo dolls in it. I decided to make one. I collected hair and personal items from others and attached them to a doll. I pretended it was a person I was angry with and stuck pins in it, hoping to cause pain or injury. It didn't work.

My mother introduced me to Zodiac signs. I looked forward to reading my daily horoscope and bought a book that taught more about it. I agreed with what it said about my personality, but I didn't understand how it knew me so well. Was my life influenced by the stars or by the God my priest spoke about? Either way, reading my horoscope was fun and easy, regardless of what it actually meant.

Like most families we participated in Halloween—a widely celebrated, culturally acceptable holiday established on fear and death.

I thought trick-or-treating was fun until my mom started searching my candy for needles and razor blades. Haunted houses were not fun. I cried and screamed my way through, terrified as I faced firsthand the scenarios from my nightmares and the gruesome movies I'd seen. Even after I became an adult, my parents still answered the door on Halloween night wearing rubber masks covered in fake blood.

The spiritual activities I took part in are considered harmless entertainment. The Ouija Board was bought at a toy store, horoscopes were in the newspaper, and everyone I knew went trick-or-treating. At the time I wasn't aware of the demonic connection. I was just a regular kid doing normal kid stuff. But my participation in these activities granted the devil intimately dangerous access into my life.

I "wish" my parents had given me the Word of God instead of those far-from-harmless fairy tales and activities. Proverb 4:23 says to "keep your heart with all diligence, for out of it spring the issues of life."

Validation

No temptation has overtaken you except such as is common to man;
but God is faithful, who will not allow you to be tempted beyond
what you are able, but with the temptation will also make
the way of escape, that you may be able to bear it.
—1 Corinthians 10:13

SATAN HAD SET ME UP for destruction. Like most people, I was unaware of his deceptions and how deeply he had infiltrated my life. By the time I entered adolescence, I had fully embraced the picture Satan had painted of me: a shameful, worthless, unlovable person with whom God was very angry.

Still hoping someone would accept me, I made friends with people whose lives were similar to mine. We understood each other's brokenness. Unfortunately, my dysfunctional friends only added fuel to the fire of destruction that was already burning within me.

I looked for love, but I didn't know what real love looked like. I ended up dating "bad boys." They didn't disappoint me—they treated me as I expected to be treated. They used me for their pleasure and then threw me out with the trash. I thought that's what I deserved, and the worse they treated me, the more attracted I was to them. These unhealthy relationships not only validated, but also reinforced my erroneous self-image.

I used alcohol and eventually drugs to dull the pain of being worthless and unloved. Beer and wine tasted bad, but the diversion appealed to me. Marijuana and hallucinogens brought the fun and laughter that was missing in my life. These substances also helped me lose my inhibitions so I could be the "real me." But the promiscuity and rebellious behaviors were not the real me. These actions came from my distorted self-image and reinforced my mistaken identity.

I looked for love, but I didn't know what real love looked like.

I spent much of my time at underage drinking parties. One night the police raided the festivities, so my parents had to pick me up at the scene. As we drove home that night, they didn't voice concern about my alcohol use. They just scolded me for inconveniencing them—they had to leave the local tavern to meet with the police.

One day I reached into my coat pocket to get my marijuana pipe—it was gone. Later when I went into the kitchen, my mom kept her back toward me and was unusually quiet. As I sat eating my snack, she turned to face me. I could see where the tears had streaked her make-up. I knew what was coming next because she tried to give me a guilt trip when she found my cigarettes months earlier.

My mom made me see a counselor in a substance abuse program. During the initial assessment, I lied about the extent of my use. I said I only used marijuana and just on weekends. My parents were told not to worry—as I was only experimenting. Dad wasn't at all concerned because he had made no real investment in my life anyway. Mom was relieved at the news, but kept a suspicious eye on me. All this meant to me was that I had to be sneakier.

My relationship with my mom continued to decline until one night it deteriorated at rapid speed. We were arguing in my bedroom; I wanted to go out with my friends and she thought I should stay home. Incensed by my disrespectful words, she slapped me in the face. Angered by the sting, I threatened to run away from home. For an instant, I saw fear in her eyes. With emotions high, she grabbed me by the shoulders and wrestled me to the floor. Pinning me down, she vowed never to let me leave the house. My eyes were oozing with hatred. My dad heard the commotion and came to investigate. He stood over us and without emotion said he didn't care what I did because he'd given up on me a long time ago. I was fifteen.

After they walked out of my room, I slammed the door shut. Feeling mortified, I called my friends to tell them I wouldn't make it to the party. A short while later, as I lay on my bed, I heard footsteps go past. My room was near the kitchen, and I heard drawers being opened and closed. I looked out my peephole under the door knob, but I could only see darkness. I waited until all was quiet and then tiptoed into the kitchen. When I turned on the small light above the sink, the knife block caught my eye. It was empty. I opened the knife drawer. It was bare. Did my mom hide all the knives from me? Was I that much of a threat to the family? No one slept well that night.

Throughout my adolescence my dad repeatedly threatened, "Get ready to pay rent on your eighteenth birthday." I would rather have died than give him anything. So immediately after my high school graduation, I moved in with my boyfriend. I had three months to spare.

Satan used the feel-good escapes of sex, alcohol, and drugs to push me further into the pit of despair. My life became twisted in a vicious cycle of destruction. As my transgressions continued, my guilt and shame increased, the added guilt and shame reinforced my negative self-image, and that led me into a more sinful lifestyle. This perpetual merry-go-round took me further and further away from God.

I was on a dead-end road to permanent despair, but God had other plans for me.

I accepted and lived in the identity Satan had crafted for me. I was on a dead-end road to permanent despair, but God had other plans for me.

God's Invitation

I will give you a new heart and put a new spirit within you; I will take the heart of stone out of your flesh and give you a heart of flesh.
—Ezekiel 36:26

AFTER I ESCAPED MY HOME, I settled down a bit. I quit all my drug use as the hallucinogens I had taken caused paranoia and flashbacks. I also limited alcohol to weekends. To pay my bills, I began flipping eggs as a line cook in a local diner. A year later I left my live-in boyfriend for another guy and got my own apartment. I jumped from one dysfunctional relationship to another until I got married at the age of twenty-four.

My husband was the brother of the boyfriend I lived with five years earlier. We hooked up at a bar where he was drowning his sorrows. He was getting divorced from his second wife. He was eight years older than me, my brother's age, so I thought he would take care of me and bring some security to my life. I hoped we'd be able to buy a house and have children someday.

Wanting to improve my life, I registered for college. Four years later I graduated and became a registered nurse. During this time my husband's alcohol consumption grew out of control. He would leave without notice and be gone for days, only to return home without any remorse. At times I'd get a phone call from the police, notifying me that my husband was in jail for driving drunk. One time I received a call from the hospital that he'd been snowmobiling and hit a parked car. He had to undergo surgery for a severely fractured leg. We had no medical insurance, so the bills mounted up. All the while his drinking continued. My dream of living happily ever after was dead. I divorced him after five painful years of marriage.

After my divorce I felt empty inside. It wasn't because my husband was gone; my situation had actually improved dramatically after leaving him. I had my own place and didn't have to worry about his whereabouts. I wasn't responsible for his actions or his bills. But still, something was missing and I didn't know what.

In an attempt to find some purpose in my life, I started jogging to improve my physical health. I went back to college and earned a master's degree in nursing. I moved from Wisconsin to Minnesota to be near my sister and her children. I took up watercolor painting and learned to downhill ski. I continued to buy expensive jewelry and clothes, hoping that would make me feel better. It didn't. I felt like I was dropping pebbles into the Grand Canyon. Nothing could fill my vast emptiness.

I was empty inside, but didn't know yet that God had placed a need inside of each of us that could only be filled by Him. I tried to fill the God-shaped hole in my heart with material possessions and my own accomplishments—but it couldn't be satisfied with those things.

One morning I said to myself, *There has got to be more to life than this. I need to go back to church.* Being new to Minnesota, I was also looking to make some friends. My sister had become a Christian a couple years earlier, so she suggested I find a Christian singles group. This seemed to fit both my needs, so I searched the Internet and found a monthly get-together for Christian singles nearby.

To my surprise it was a non-denominational church that held a Friday night service as part of their singles ministry. The sanctuary seated about three thousand people and had three large screens behind the stage. Musicians were strumming guitars and singing worship songs. The lights were turned dim, making it easy to slip into a seat without being noticed.

Many in attendance raised their hands, hollered halleluiah, and whispered words of love to Jesus. I had stumbled into unknown territory, and though my natural instinct was to run for the door, I decided to try to fit in by singing along. After the music ended, a woman in her forties got on stage. Her jeans were snug and her shirt was modest but trendy. I thought she was going to introduce a pastor, but she started to preach. As she spoke the group took notes and shouted out Amen in agreement.

Near the end of the pastor's sermon she said, "God is love. And if you're looking for love, you're looking for God." I scoffed. Love was the last thing I needed. But at the same time, I had a longing for this type of love, and right there in that sanctuary, I was drawn into the arms of Jesus.

When I got home, my sister was in the kitchen cleaning up. We sat on the couch to discuss my adventure. "You wouldn't believe this place, Dawn. It had a huge sanctuary with a beautiful stage and big viewing screens. There were a couple hundred single men and women openly worshiping God in a way I've never seen before. The sermon was like nothing I've ever heard and the pastor talked so enthusiastically about Jesus." I shrugged, "What's so special about Jesus?"

Having accepted Christ as her Savior in recent years, Dawn was able to explain it to me. She said, "When Adam sinned, mankind became separated from God. To restore our relationship with a holy God, our sins had to be removed. Since we couldn't do it ourselves, God sent Jesus. When Jesus sacrificed His sinless life on the cross, He took our sin upon Himself and gave us His righteousness. But this exchange only occurs for us personally if we believe that Jesus is God's son, He died for our sins, and He rose again. If we believe that, then our sins are forgiven and washed away. This makes it possible for us to have a relationship with God and go to Heaven when we die."

"Really?" I asked. "That's it? You mean I don't have to earn my way into Heaven?"

She replied, "You can't earn salvation, it's a gift from God. All you have to do is receive it."

I pondered everything I had experienced that night. Could this actually be true? Could it truly be that simple? The next day I looked through the visitor's packet I had picked up at church the night before. Inside was a booklet titled, "Have You Heard the Good News?"

I had finally found the unconditional love and acceptance I'd been searching for my entire life.

As I sat on my bed and read, it confirmed what Dawn told me the night before, citing Bible verses to prove it.

On the last page was an invitation for me to say a prayer proclaiming Jesus as my Lord and Savior. I fell to my knees beside the bed and read out loud the words on the page, meaning them with all my heart. I instantly felt happy and peaceful inside. I had finally found the unconditional love and acceptance I'd been searching for my entire life.

Over the next few months, I fell head-over-heels in love with Jesus. Like a bride on her honeymoon, I couldn't get enough of Him. I went to church every time the doors were open. I joined Bible studies, did street evangelism, and became involved with community outreach. I was baptized in the Holy Spirit and received the ability to speak in tongues. I experienced God's sweet presence and was filled with His joy, peace, and love—things I didn't even know existed.

As I read my Bible one day, I came to John 8:1-11. In this passage the religious leaders of Jesus's day brought a woman caught in adultery to Him. The law declared she must be stoned, but they wanted to know what Jesus had to say. Jesus said to them, "He who is without sin among you, let him throw a stone at her first" (v.7). Being convicted by their conscience, they went out one by one (v.9). When they were all gone, Jesus said to the woman, "Neither do I condemn you; go and sin no more" (v.11).

I felt that God was telling me that I had some sins in my life. I didn't know what they were, but I understood deep in my soul that He was not condemning me for them. Sure enough, over the next few months, the Holy Spirit began to convict me of my sinful behaviors. He started with my love for money.

I had decided to become a member of the church I'd been attending. During the new member's class, the pastor taught about tithing. I concluded that I couldn't afford to give 10 percent of my income to God because I was saving all the money I could to buy a house.

All of a sudden, God seemed distant, as if a wall had been erected between us. Confused about what I was feeling, I called my new friend, Lisa. She was the leader of my Alpha group, a class that teaches the basics of Christianity, and I knew I could confide in her. I explained to Lisa that my heart sensed that God was far away. She told me that sin is the only thing that can separate us from God. I understood what she was saying, but couldn't think of anything I did to cause this.

The following Sunday, as the pastor took the offering, God opened my eyes to the cause of the problem. I had heard what the Bible says about tithing, but when I refused to do it, I was being disobedient. I concluded that I would rather live in God's presence than have any amount of money. From then on, every time I got paid, I gladly tithed 10 percent of my earnings to my church. Also, my mindset about expensive clothes and jewelry started to change. I still liked to dress nicely, but it wasn't so much a part of my identity anymore.

Once I made the decision to tithe, the barrier between God and I was removed, and I could sense Him with me again. The Bible says God never leaves us nor forsakes us (Heb. 13:5). When God felt distant, He was still with me, but He was further away. I had inadvertently pushed myself away from God because of my disobedience. When I yielded to God's authority, I came back where I belonged—close to Him.

A few weeks later, the Holy Spirit dealt with me about the television shows and movies I watched. One night my sister walked in the room to find me watching *The Bachelor*, a reality television show about a man tasked with choosing the one he would marry out of a pool of beautiful, but mostly shallow women. With disgust on her face, Dawn asked, "Why are you watching that junk?"

I didn't have a good answer. But her words stirred something deep inside of me, and as I flipped through the channels I realized I couldn't find anything worthwhile. I turned it off. The very next night, I started to watch a movie I'd rented. The vulgar language and the sexual promiscuity offended me for the first time ever. I could no longer watch such things. I stopped watching television and movies altogether.

Another area of my life that needed adjustment was my alcohol use. I was still a "social drinker," having a glass of wine after work or a drink or two on the weekend. One night as I talked to a friend at church, he told me he didn't drink alcohol because he thought it impaired his ability to hear from God. That made sense to me. I decided to quit—right after I drank my last two wine coolers.

That weekend I opened a Seagram's fuzzy navel. As I was about to take the first sip, I felt an unnatural struggle within myself. I couldn't raise the bottle to my mouth. I just sat and stared at it. My mind told me to drink it, but my spirit said no. After a short dispute my spirit won the battle, and I poured them both down the drain.

I am pleased to say that God instantly took away my desire for alcohol. In fact, He made it so repulsive to me that I can't drink it anymore—not even if I wanted to.

As a new believer, I didn't immediately recognize all the things that were offensive to God. I wasn't aware I had to make changes until God confronted me on each one. He graciously showed me that He wanted me to change my old habits, to get rid of the ungodly stuff in my life. God wanted to remove every influence that interfered with my relationship with Him.

I was looking only at my behaviors. I had no idea that my heart was badly wounded and scarred.

God made it easy to change. What I had previously enjoyed just no longer appealed to me, and in the case of television and alcohol, I developed a strong aversion to both. His conviction of my sins were certainly not like the condemnation I'd felt in the past.

A year into my walk with God, I believed that He had finished His work in me. I thought I was all cleaned up because the external stuff, the most obvious offenses were gone. But I was looking only at my behaviors. I had no idea that my heart was badly wounded and scarred.

Even so, I was not so damaged that God couldn't repair my injuries. Like a skillful surgeon, He could gently cleanse and mend my wounded heart. However, for my heart to heal, I had to allow God to put me into His refining fire.

According to Merriam-Webster, refine means "to reduce to a pure state, to improve by pruning or polishing, or to become free from what is coarse or vulgar." When gold is refined, fire is used to remove the impurities within it. This process is repetitive and time consuming, but the end product is pure gold. Just like that, God wanted to use His godly fire and refine me into the purest gold. Malachi 3:3 says, "He will sit as a refiner and a purifier of silver; He will purify the sons of Levi, and purge them as gold and silver."

I went through the first firing process when God transformed my behaviors. But things hidden deep in my heart still needed to be burned away. My family, my childhood church, and our culture had tarnished my heart.

My refinement could not take place through sermons or Bible studies. I had to go through difficult situations and endure afflictions in order for God to change me in His perfect way, in His perfect timing. But I wasn't ready for the fire. So God waited and watched a harvest of adversity grow in my life.

The Subtle Pulling Away

But make sure that you don't get so absorbed and exhausted in
taking care of all your day-by-day obligations that you lose track of
the time and doze off, oblivious to God.
—Romans 13:11 (MES)

IN MY NIGHTLY PRAYER TIMES, I began asking God what He wanted me to do with my life. Months went by without a response. Finally, I heard God's soft voice speak to my spirit, *Adopt a child*. I was stunned. With my nursing background, I thought He would ask me to do a medical mission trip. Adopting a child had never before entered my mind!

As I mulled this over God whispered, *Hannah* and *China*. I had no further qualms. My mission was clear.

I hesitated to tell family and friends about this word from the Lord because I was single and concerned about how it would be received. I told Dawn first. She just smiled and said, "You'll be a great mom." This gave me courage to tell my mother, but I was glad I could deliver the news to her by phone just in case it didn't go well. Surprisingly, she was very supportive. I told a few of my close friends at church. They questioned if this was right for me.

I started the arduous process. I chose a Christian agency that did adoptions exclusively from China. Anyone who has adopted knows that obtaining documents and filling out the paperwork takes many months to complete. While I waited for a call from the agency, I painted and decorated my spare bedroom. I covered the walls in bright yellow, and a friend gave me the crib that her adopted daughter had outgrown. I bought clothes and toys and prepared as best I could. I felt as excited as any expectant mother!

I kept attending church services and Bible studies where I continued to gain knowledge about God. This was a good start, but God wanted me to know Him personally and intimately. I thought I did. Along the way, I mistook dramatic encounters with God, such as His manifest presence or a prophetic word, as intimacy. I unknowingly substituted these experiences for a close relationship because my wounded heart rendered me either unwilling or unable to have a deep union with God. I also did what every person who avoids intimacy does: I kept myself busy.

In the church, busyness is disguised because we call it serving God. After all, it seemed like a great way to show God my love. I became a teacher's assistant and eventually a teacher in the church's preschool room. I helped with computer check-in for the children's ministry, passed baskets to collect tithes, cleaned the sanctuary, and packed boxes of food for the needy. I volunteered out of my thankfulness to God, but my heart's hidden motive was to avoid getting too close to Him. I did have some prayer time, but to prevent real intimacy I used a good and acceptable excuse—I did His work.

Serving God, instead of spending time with Him, seemed like an acceptable use of my time, but it would eventually cause me trouble. It was like the disparity between knowing about God and knowing God. I should have volunteered in addition to my personal time with God, not to replace it.

Jesus addressed this in Luke 10:39-42, when He visited two sisters, Martha and Mary. Mary sat at Jesus's feet and listened to His words. But Martha was "distracted with much serving" (v. 40). She said to Jesus, "Lord, do you not care that my sister has left me to serve alone? Therefore tell her to help me" (v. 40).

Jesus said to her, "Martha, Martha, you are worried and troubled about many things. But one thing is needed, and Mary has chosen that good part, which will not be taken away from her" (v. 41-42).

Jesus said that Mary made the better choice. Unfortunately, I was like Martha, frantically running around doing work for the Lord. But God wanted more than my service. He wanted my full attention and my whole heart.

But God wanted more than my service. He wanted my full attention and my whole heart.

Three years into my walk with God, my life changed from busyness in the church to busyness at home. The adoption agency called. Shao Fan Gao was ten months old and her pictures and medical information were in the mail! I was excited, but admit that I had a mixture of emotions. I felt relieved that the waiting period was finally over, yet I had trepidation about the upcoming travel. After waiting two more months for China to give us permission to travel there, my sister, Dawn, and I boarded the plane. Twelve hours after arriving, a Chinese nanny placed my long-awaited daughter in my arms. It was just four days before her first birthday. Hannah had a fever and smelled as if she'd never had a bath, but I fell in love with her. She didn't fuss or cry and seemed to enjoy the commotion that enveloped her.

Our time in China was spent fulfilling adoption requirements, such as getting Hannah a medical exam, visiting the embassy, and filling out more required paperwork. We also enjoyed some local shopping and sightseeing. Most importantly was our bonding time.

On our return trip to the States, I was completely exhausted. Fortunately, I had arranged to take a couple months off work to adjust to my new life as a mom. During this time Hannah kept me busy. We had medical appointments for ear infections and feeding difficulties. I helped her overcome her fear of sleeping in her crib, taking baths, and even being outside. I had little time or energy left at the end of the day, so I often had a sink full of dirty bottles, a garbage can stuffed with stinky diapers, and toys scattered all over the floor.

Becoming a single mom of a one-year-old drastically changed my life. I had to resign from my church commitments and all other volunteering. My well-intentioned community outreach screeched to a halt.

I reduced my church attendance to one service a week, as Hannah cried when I took her to the nursery. If I got to sit in the service at all, it became more of a rest from Hannah than to grow in the Lord. My evenings were too busy to attend Bible study groups, but I tried to read my Bible after Hannah went to bed. Unfortunately, I was always so tired that my eyes merely grazed over the words.

My prayer time became nearly extinct. The few times I did pray the devil whispered, *I'm too tired* or *I'm so tired* in my ear. His words made me feel more tired and I told myself I would pray with more enthusiasm the next day. I believed those thoughts of tiredness were my own because they made sense—I *was* tired.

Eventually, I adjusted to my dual role of breadwinner and caregiver. Rather than renew my relationship with God, I used the excuse that I was too busy and too tired. I became complacent. I thought God could wait. After all, He'd called me to this responsibility.

Even after Hannah outgrew her need for bottles and diapers, I still spent very little time with God. I went to church every Saturday night, read my Bible sporadically, and prayed occasionally, but it wasn't enough to develop my relationship with God. Not only was I not growing in God, but my spirit became weak. I no longer had the intimate connection I had with Him before. I didn't develop or foster my identity in Christ and I never made it back into the Refiner's fire. All this enabled the devil to slowly pull me away from God.

I repeatedly asked God, "Where is my joy?"

He didn't answer. Either He had stopped listening or He didn't care, or both. When I prayed, it seemed as though I was talking to a wall. Eventually prayer became just another task.

My heart had grown angry with God for giving me the difficult assignment of being a single mom. I loved Hannah and she brought me much pleasure, but I was often overloaded with the responsibilities of my job, our household, and raising a child on my own. If I had been close to God, I would have looked to Him for help and strength. Instead, I began to blame God for my problems.

One night as I sat at my desk, the devil whispered in my ear, *You don't really need God that much, do you?* I didn't accept or reject these words. I didn't agree or disagree. I just carried on.

The Wake-up Call

THE DEVIL HAD ORCHESTRATED my pulling away, but it only occurred because I allowed it. I let life's circumstances interfere with the activities that kept me spiritually strong. In my weakened state, I stumbled around in the darkness and couldn't see how far from God I had wandered. Two poignant events shed light on my condition and allowed me to see more clearly where I was at.

The first occurred at a department store as I shopped for pajamas for Hannah. The pajamas were sold as a set, but the pants were too long. I took two sets apart and made a new pair that fit her just right. That left a mismatched set that the store would be unable to sell.

I knew what I did was wrong. I didn't care.

> I let life's circumstances interfere with the activities that kept me spiritually strong.

31

A week later, when I woke up, I realized that I'd had an evil dream, but I couldn't remember any details. As I got Hannah ready for preschool, she looked at me and said, "Mommy, you look scary." She covered her face with her hands and hid in a corner.

After I dropped her off, I thought about what she'd said and what it could mean. Could it be connected to the dream I had the night before? Then I remembered the pajama incident. Not only had I knowingly done something wrong, but more concerning was that it didn't bother me. I investigated the evidence: my heart was no longer sensitive to the Holy Spirit, I'd had an evil dream, and I looked scary to my daughter. With this, I concluded that I needed to get back to God.

That night I developed a strategy for getting closer to God. I decided I would replace the time I had been spending surfing the Internet and talking on the phone to family and friends with prayer and Bible study. My church had just started "Revival Wednesdays," and I decided to attend.

Those services were exactly what I needed. They focused on repentance for being lukewarm toward God, regretting our apathy with the desire to change. We were given the opportunity to ask God for forgiveness and start fresh with a revived relationship. That's just what I did. I spent the next two Wednesday nights at church on my knees, crying and repenting for leaving God. I also prayed at home and asked God to forgive me.

One night as I told God, "All I want is you," I heard, *What if He doesn't take you back?* I was stunned. I had never thought of that possibility! Over the next couple of days, the devil continued to hammer my mind with questions and doubts about my salvation. I couldn't resolve them within myself, and I was tormented by the possibility that God might not forgive me and I would be sentenced to Hell for eternity.

One night, as I writhed in bed tortured by these thoughts, the devil told me to jump off my second-story deck! As he urged me on, I disputed with myself. How could I live a normal life knowing I would go to Hell when I died? But I couldn't jump. If I did, I would go to Hell right now. Was it worse to live in mental anguish as I waited to go to Hell or to go to Hell now? After much debate, I concluded that if I was alive there was still a chance God would forgive me.

In the morning I called Ed, a pastor friend of mine. I told him that I had drifted away from God, and I wasn't sure if I still belonged to Him. I was afraid that God had turned His back on me. Ed quoted some relevant Bible verses about forgiveness and reassured me of God's goodness. I felt a little better, but the tranquility didn't last long.

That evening, the devil reminded me of Hebrews 6:4-6, which says, "It is impossible for those who were once enlightened, and have tasted the heavenly gift, and have become partakers of the Holy Spirit, and have tasted the good word of God and the powers of the age to come, if they fall away, to renew them again to repentance, since they crucify again for themselves the Son of God, and put Him to open shame."

That sounded like me. I'd once had a vibrant relationship with God, but then I wandered off. How could I be renewed when the Bible said it was impossible?

Over the next couple of weeks, I struggled with intense fear. I was afraid for both my spiritual and physical welfare. Anxiety was causing my stomach to be upset on a daily basis. Every ounce of food I managed to eat was a chore to get down, so I lived mostly on high-calorie protein drinks. I'd lost almost ten pounds, and I was not overweight to start. At times I saw blood in the toilet and suspected

I'd developed an ulcer. I popped Tums medicine throughout the day, trying to gain some relief. It didn't seem to help much.

I did everything I could to relieve the anxiety. I looked for Bible verses about God's mercy and forgiveness, and I repeatedly reminded myself of these truths. When I came across scriptures about His wrath and judgment, I closed my eyes and quickly turned the page, telling myself those were not for me.

I called my church for help and talked with a pastor. She said I needed a revelation of God's grace. She recommended I read *The Father Loves You* by Ed Piorek. In this book he talks about the prodigal son, and as I read about him, I saw myself.

The parable, told in Luke 15:11-32, is about a man with two sons. The younger son asks his father for his share of the inheritance and then goes to a far-off country where he wastes his possessions with riotous living. A famine comes to the land and he ends up feeding swine. He would have been grateful just to eat their food. When he comes to his senses, he heads home with the hope of becoming his father's hired servant. When he is still a long way off, his father runs out to meet him, puts a robe and ring on him, and holds an impromptu yet elaborate celebration in his son's honor.

I had always thought of a prodigal son as someone who went out into the world to lead a sinful life. But that is not the only path to the pigsty. I was in the pigsty alongside the prodigal son, and not because I ran off to engage in lustful activities. I got there by being overly busy and complacent in my relationship with God. The prodigal son's motivation was self-pleasure and he deliberately walked away from his father. My catalyst was busyness and fatigue and I slowly lost my way from home.

As I neared the end of the story in the book, tears streamed down my face. I cried to God, "I just want to come home. I just want to come home."

Right then, God's sweet presence descended and rested upon me. Through my sobs I heard myself say, "I am accepted in the Beloved" over and over. The Holy Spirit had spoken through me and told me I was forgiven and that God accepted me—just as Ephesians 1:6 says: "To the praise of the glory of His grace, by which He made us accepted in the Beloved."

This display of God's love calmed my fears—for a while. But the devil was relentless. He continued to trigger landmines buried in my heart, setting the uncertainty of my salvation on fire again. Once more, insecurities and anxiety surged. I was destined for the night of the crisis.

On the night of the crisis, the devil found me in the second-floor guest room of my parents' apartment building. He pounded my mind with lies that God had not forgiven me and I was destined for Hell. He tried to kill me by filling me with an overwhelming urge to fling myself over the balcony. After barely surviving the night, I called my pastor friend Ed, who agreed to meet with me and pray.

With Hannah at my parents' place and my sister on her way to care for her, I drove to my house to meet with Ed—and with God.

Who is My Father?

When you pray, go into your room, and when you have shut your door,
pray to your Father who is in the secret place...
—Matthew 6:6

ED ARRIVED AT MY HOUSE shortly after I did. We had been friends for almost six years, but we hadn't talked much in the last year or so. When I opened the door for him, I instantly felt embarrassed about the mess my life was in. I lowered my eyes to the floor as I greeted him.

To keep out the cold February air, I quickly ushered him in. As he took his coat and shoes off, I breathed a sigh of relief that help had arrived. Ed was in his sixties and had been like a father or older brother to me. Ed had the gift of availability because he wasn't married and was pastoring only a very small church.

As we descended the stairs of my split-level townhouse, I realized that though we had both been in prayer groups, we had never prayed together. I felt uneasy, but I knew I needed help.

I figured the lower-level room would be best for praying. With my computer desk tucked in one corner and Hannah's kitchen set and puppet house in the others, there was an area in the middle for us to use. The sun reflecting off the snow was bright, so I pulled the shade on the patio door.

As I did that, Ed said, "I keep my eyes open and walk around while I pray. My eyes are open when I talk to people, so why should I close them when I speak to God? I walk because it keeps me from being distracted, and I can concentrate on God's voice better. I think you should try it."

"Okay," I replied. I sometimes prayed while driving, so keeping my eyes open was not new for me. While I didn't usually walk around during prayer, I also didn't sit with my hands folded and head bowed either. I was open to anything, besides, my expectation was that Ed would just pray over me and then leave.

Ed started to walk around the room's perimeter and I followed behind him. He asked God to help me, and since I didn't know what else to do, I quietly prayed in tongues. I secretly hoped that God wouldn't reject me, sentence me to Hell, or kill me on the spot.

After a few minutes, Ed switched to tongues as well. Then he started getting revelation knowledge from God and relayed it to me as it came. "God has revealed to me that something is out of place in your life. As you've attempted to understand the status of your salvation, your faith has moved from your heart to your mind. But your logical mind can't determine your salvation because faith is supernatural. It can't be proved or disproved."

Ed stopped walking and looked me in the eyes. He said, "By questioning your salvation, you've engaged with the devil. You've given him your ear and therefore permission to speak into your life."

I looked at the floor and asked, "What do I do now?"

"Rather than quarrel with the devil about your salvation, you need to disengage your mind and deflect his comments with your faith. He can't argue against, or reason with faith—it's unreasonable. Romans 1:17 says the just shall live by faith. It doesn't say to live by logic or reason. To gain the strength you need to live by faith, you have to build yourself up by praying in the Holy Spirit more, as Jude 1:20 says.

"Also, by questioning your salvation, you've proved that you have more confidence in God's rejection of you than you have of His acceptance. Before you can receive God's acceptance, you first have to receive His love."

I replied, "In my mind I know that God loves me, but I guess I haven't accepted His love into my heart."

"You fight against God's love because you think He's unsafe. You've been hurt a lot in the past, and you assume God is like everyone else. You think if you accept God's love, you'll become vulnerable to Him. It seems wise to keep Him at arm's length. But by doing so you've closed your heart to Him."

You fight against God's love because you think He's unsafe.

"That's the last thing I want. How do I accept God's love, rather than merely acknowledge it?" I asked.

"That will come in time. In contrast, you need to acknowledge the devil, but not accept anything from him. You can start doing that immediately."

I gave Ed a puzzled look and so he continued to explain.

"When Satan came to Jesus in the wilderness, Jesus acknowledged him. Jesus didn't accept or submit to what Satan said, and He didn't debate or get into a conversation with him. Jesus's only response was 'It is written,' followed by the Word of God" (Matt. 4:1-10). "That was His only communication with Satan."

"Can I use this same technique to subdue the devil?" I asked.

"Yes. Rather than talk *with* the devil, you need to be like Jesus and speak *to* the devil with 'It is written' followed by the appropriate scripture. Just because your mind hears and acknowledges the devil's accusations, you don't have to accept them into your heart."

Ed continued, "To help refute the devil's lies and strengthen your faith, I want you to proclaim to God and to yourself what you believe and accept."

"I'm so tired and confused by the lies that I don't even know what that is," I admitted.

"I'll help you," Ed replied. "Repeat after me: I accept that God loves me the way I am. I accept that my salvation is real. I choose to believe what is in my heart and not what I hear in my head. I choose to believe what God says about me, not what I think or feel, or what the devil says."

I spoke with a shaky confidence, yet I sensed a fighting attitude emerge within me. As we continued, a surge of power seemed to reignite the flame of my faith. I started to declare my beliefs with conviction, and when a small smile appeared on my face, Ed knew our session was done.

As we left our prayer room, I felt a glimmer of hope. God hadn't rejected me after all. On the contrary, He had taught me, with Ed's help, how to fight the devil! Ed and I went upstairs. I poured us each a glass of water and we sat on the couch to rest. I noticed some of the tenseness in my body was gone. I confessed to Ed, "I didn't expect God to talk to me, much less give me words of wisdom."

"I didn't anticipate being a conduit for God's teachings," he shared. "That was amazing!"

Little did we know that this was just the beginning of God's handiwork. We would spend many more hours wearing a rut in the carpet while God imparted life-changing truths.

The next morning I wasn't ready to go to work, so I called in sick for the last two days of the week. I walked into Hannah's room, and as I sat on her empty bed, I realized I should let my mom know that I was all right. I couldn't tell her I was engaged in spiritual warfare because she wouldn't understand. But I called her and said I was having some emotional problems, and Ed was helping me work through them. She offered more help if I needed it and after a few minutes of superficial conversation, we said goodbye.

Later that morning my sister stopped by my house. She came to pick up some clothes and other essentials for Hannah. I sat on the couch as Dawn packed what she needed. I didn't want to talk to her about my situation. When Satan had first brought doubts about my salvation, I confided in her that I felt insecure. She discredited my feelings when she tersely replied, "You know God forgives us." She didn't understand what I was going through, so I didn't tell her that my fear and anxiety had worsened.

I also avoided her because I felt guilty. I had imposed custody of Hannah on her the day before, without warning or explanation. She had three kids and a life of her own and wasn't all that keen to add more. Even so, Dawn was gracious toward me. She would take care of Hannah for as long as I needed her to because that's what sisters do.

As we stood at the front door, I reached out and hugged her. Through my tears I blubbered, "Take care of my little girl." She assured me that she would and then promptly left.

Since I was home alone and eager for help, I called Ed and asked him to come over to pray. He agreed and came after lunch. We went down to our prayer room and got into our pattern of walking in a circle, with Ed in front and me following him. We hadn't been praying long when Ed said, "Unforgiveness. There's a seed of unforgiveness."

I stopped in my tracks. In my mind I saw myself lying face down on a cot. A man stood over me, striking my back with a whip. As he whipped me, someone else stood by in the distance and watched. Whoever it was didn't approve, yet he or she didn't intervene. Did that person symbolize God? All I knew was my heart ached. Through tears I cried, "It hurts so much, it hurts so much."

"Don't be afraid to go there," I heard Ed say. "We'll do this together. Open the eyes of your heart and see it."

The pain in my heart intensified, and I wailed uncontrollably.

"There is nothing hidden that will not be revealed," Ed said. "Take it in! Pull up the tares! Yes, it is so!"

I slumped to the floor in agony. I realized the man in my vision was my dad. Though he had never physically hurt me, my dad had inflicted me with emotional wounds. I lay there and sobbed until I had nothing left inside. Ed covered my limp body with a blanket and sat on the floor beside me.

When Satan feeds us a lie and we accept it into our hearts, a seed is planted.

After a few minutes, I sat up and told Ed about the vision I experienced. He handed me a tissue. "When you were crying, God told me that when Satan feeds us a lie and we accept it into our hearts, a seed is planted. Initially, a seed doesn't appear threatening. We can't even tell it's there—until it starts to grow. The seed grows into a thistle, thorn, or root of bitterness," Ed said.

"Is God saying a seed of unforgiveness was planted in my heart years ago, and now it's grown into a thorn?" I asked.

"Yes. But in Christ you have redemption from all of the devil's work, including the impact it has on your heart, the reactions it produces in you, and even his work that becomes a part of who you are.

But we need to be careful. Matthew 13:29 says that pulling up tares, that is thistles, thorns, and roots of bitterness, without God's help is dangerous for the wheat—in this case your heart."

"So how do I get rid of the pain? What are the reactions that my heart is having and what part of me is the devil's work?" I asked.

"I don't know. But God does. I believe He wants the tares in your heart removed, and He will help you gently pull them out."

We stood up, and as we prayed revelation knowledge flowed from Ed. "You've put yourself on probation with God because you believe in performance-based acceptance. You allowed yourself to be pulled away by Satan, so you think your performance has fallen below standards. But you're the one who established those standards, not God. He has no such requirement for you."

"Why can't I have a standard for me in my relationship with God?" I asked.

"Look where it's gotten you. Grasp the reality that you can't earn God's love because He loves you without conditions. He approves you based on Jesus's work on the cross. He accepts you beyond your ability to understand, and your understanding isn't required. You can never earn the place of acceptance He has already given you. You've been bought and paid for; you're already owned by God. First Corinthians 6:20 says so. You are accepted in the Beloved no matter what you do, and your imperfections cannot disqualify you."

You are accepted in the Beloved no matter what you do, and your imperfections cannot disqualify you.

Though these words came from Ed's mouth, I knew God was speaking to me. I still had anxiety about my salvation, but I started to comprehend that God accepted and loved me with all my faults and failures, and the knowledge of His love moved from my head into my heart. I took myself off probation. I was ready to receive His unconditional love and acceptance.

I called my sister's house to talk to Hannah. "Hi sweetie. How are you doing?"

"I miss you and I wanna come home," Hannah whined.

"I miss you too, but you can't come home yet. Mama's sick and I need some time to get better."

"Okay. I hope you get better fast Mama," Hannah said.

I felt sad that Hannah wasn't at home, but I had to take care of myself before I could take care of her. That much was clear.

After I hung up with Hannah, I called Ed and asked him to come over and pray with me again. When he arrived we got into our now-familiar prayer formation and started praying in tongues. After a short time, Ed stopped walking and looked at me. "Three times you've said, 'You are mine' to God."

I smiled. I'd never had my prayer language interpreted before. I switched to English and said to God, "You are my Father."

Ed winced. "When you said those words, my spirit felt God cringe."

My stomach tightened out of fear. "Does God not want to be my Father? Don't I belong to Him?"

"God cringed because you've transposed your earthly father's image onto Him. It's like you've taken a snapshot of your dad and put it on God's face. And not just your dad's face—his voice, character, personality, and standards. You've imposed his whole image onto God."

As I stood there trying to make sense of this, Ed started walking around me praying in tongues. Then he said, "God is pulling a page out of your book and He's going to rewrite it!"

Surely Ed had lost his mind. At best he hadn't heard God accurately. I didn't believe what he was saying about my dad and God because I couldn't see what I had done.

In my defense I said, "I can relate to Jesus. He's my Savior and my friend. I love Him."

"It's because you had a brother like that. You see Jesus in the same way you saw your brother."

Filled with God's power, those words pierced my heart. I fell to the floor clutching my chest. Rather than focus on what was said, all I could do was lay there and say, "I'm so glad I'm saved," over and over.

When my elation passed, I realized I had undeniable evidence that what God revealed through Ed was true. I *had* painted my dad's face on God, just like I'd transferred my brother's persona onto Jesus. That explained why I focused most of my devotion toward Jesus, because He was safe—like my brother. I avoided God because I thought He was like my dad.

Ed said, "God wants you to know that He is not like your earthly father, and He never will be."

I avoided God because I thought He was like my dad.

Before that could fully sink in, Ed continued, "You have a skewed picture of yourself as well. Your self-portrait has been pieced together from lies that you've accepted as truth. To correct your picture, you have to put the lies in a casket, close the lid, and bury the person you've always thought you were. Only then can you become your true self.

"Remember the prodigal son? When he came home, he was wearing filthy rags. Because of his time spent in the pig pen, he didn't look like his father's son. But when his father saw him, he ran out and put the best robe on him and a ring on his finger. These symbolized the father's power, authority, and unconditional love. God has done the same for you, but in your eyes you still live in your trough-stained rags. Those mud-covered clothes can't be worn in God's kingdom, and you can't wear a robe of righteousness over them. You have to take the rags off. This will require a paradigm shift. You need to see yourself as God sees you."

"How do I do that?" I asked.

"The first steps are for you to understand and acknowledge that you are not who you think you are. You're a fraud, and everything you know about yourself comes from a fraudulent perspective. That's why you still wear the rags, because your beliefs about yourself are wrong."

My mind spun. If I wasn't who I thought I was, then who was I? I told Ed, "I want to see myself as God sees me, but I'm afraid I can't."

"That's because your skewed picture is so familiar that it seems impossible to change. But in Mark 10:27, Jesus said, 'With God all things are possible.' Even so, this transformation won't happen overnight. It'll probably take years."

"Let's look at Matthew 23:9," Ed suggested.

Using my Bible software program, I had it on the computer screen in a few seconds. It says, "Do not call anyone on earth your father; for One is your Father, He who is in Heaven."

Speaking in truth Ed said, "Your dad is not your real father. He did not create you. God created you—in His image and likeness. When God adopted you, as Ephesians 1:5 says, you lost every oppressive tie with your dad. You are no longer his daughter and you shouldn't be dressed in the rags he made you wear. Part of the reason you continue to wear the rags is because you hold your dad in high esteem. That's why you've believed every demeaning word he's ever said about you."

My throat tightened and my vision became blurred by the moisture in my eyes.

Ed kept pressing, "You honor your dad's ugly words, even though they're wrong."

"His words are not true!" I yelled through my tears.

"In Revelation 3:9, Jesus said to the church in Philadelphia, 'Indeed, I will make those of the synagogue of Satan, who say they are Jews and are not, but lie—indeed I will make them come and worship before your feet, and to know that I have loved you.' Likewise, someday your dad will acknowledge that God rejoices over you, whereas he doesn't. God will make him show respect to you. The child abuser will be made to kneel before his righteous daughter."

With Hannah at my sister's house, I didn't have to worry about being mentally alert during the night, so I started taking sleeping pills again. This allowed me to get enough sleep to safely return to my job as a nurse practitioner. I was only gone from work for a few days, and no one seemed to miss me. None of my coworkers were Christians, so I didn't take the time to confide in them. They had no idea of the nightmare I was living.

The anxiety persisted. I managed during the day, as my job distracted me, but my pounding heart made it impossible to sleep at night without the medication. This anxiety had to go. I couldn't live like this. I wanted my girl Hannah to come home.

I desperately wanted to get better, so I asked Ed to pray with me after work. When he arrived, he prayed, asking God to reveal why I was still filled with anxiety.

After a few minutes of praying, Ed looked up a verse. "Colossians 3:15 says, 'Let the peace of God rule in your hearts.' God's peace occurs in our hearts, but anxiety is in our head. It's like a mental disease. That verse in Colossians says we are to *let* the peace of God rule in our hearts. That means you can choose to have peace and joy or fear and anxiety."

I shot Ed a wounded look. Did he think I was *choosing* this anxiety?

Ed didn't notice my reaction. He was looking up another Bible verse. "In John 14:27, Jesus said, 'Peace I leave with you. My peace I give to you; not as the world gives do I give to you. Let not your heart be troubled, neither let it be afraid.' This peace is the tranquil state of a soul assured of its salvation through Christ, having nothing to fear from God."

I confessed, "I still don't have peace about my salvation, in part because the devil continues to whisper a steady flow of fear-producing "what if" questions. Such as, what if God changes His mind about me? What if God really doesn't love me?"

Ed replied, "These questions are mental arguments that have no real answers. When you try to answer the devil's inquiries, you give him power to instill anxiety into you. To prevent anxiety from coming in and for the peace of God to rule in your heart, you have to apply the truth. This entails knowing God's Word and speaking it." Ed stopped walking, looked me in the eyes, and said, "Describe to me who you are."

> To prevent anxiety from coming in and for the peace of God to rule in your heart, you have to apply the truth.

I had no idea. "I know I'm not who I thought I was, but I don't know who I am," I said as I realized I was having an identity crisis of gigantic proportions. I could no longer rely on who I thought I was. I was forced to investigate who I am in Christ.

"To know who you are, you first have to understand who God is. First John 4:8 tells us that God is love. First Corinthians 13:4-8 explains that love is patient and kind, it does not envy, it isn't arrogant or selfish or provoked to anger, it takes no account of evil, and it rejoices in the truth."

To know who you are, you first have to understand who God is.

I had read those verses before, so I knew what the Bible said about love. But I hadn't put love on God's face—or on mine.

"I know who you are," Ed said as he sat down at my desk. "You're a daughter of God." He paused. "But being a daughter hurts."

Tears welled up in my eyes. God had pierced my heart with another truth from my past. It was painful to be my dad's daughter.

Ed explained, "To avoid further hurt you've learned to guard your heart. This prevents God from developing a Father-daughter relationship with you." He stood up and said, "It's like there is a fish hook in your heart. And this hook has to be removed."

"That sounds painful," I said warily.

"To avoid ripping your heart, it has to be pushed in a bit further, turned sideways, and then pulled out. God has already grabbed hold of that hook, and He clearly plans to take it out."

I felt we were making good progress, but in the meantime I still had to battle the devil's "what if" questions. Ed offered to help me make a list of God's attributes, so I could have them in writing when I needed to focus on that.

Like an eager student, I grabbed a notepad and pen from my desk.

Ed prompted, "God is . . ."

I closed my eyes and tried to remember what the Bible says about God. "Love. Merciful. Holy. Powerful."

As I wrote these down, Ed added, "Beautiful. Perfect. Your rock. Your strong tower. Your Father." After a pause he said, "We should also list who you are in Christ. You are . . ."

Recalling our recent conversations, I answered, "Accepted in the Beloved. A daughter of the Most High God."

"Yes," Ed agreed. "And you are fearfully and wonderfully made. Victorious. Filled with faith."

"I'm beginning to get a glimpse of myself as the daughter of a powerful yet tender and loving Father!" I exclaimed.

Ed replied, "Your heavenly Father is to be obeyed. But He is also your Daddy and you can know Him intimately enough to sit on His lap."

I loved that image.

"In order for intimacy to develop between you and God, you have to spend time with Him. That's the only way you'll get to know Him well enough that you can trust Him with your heart."

I had begun to take off some of my dirty rags, and I tossed a few pieces of my old picture into the casket that day. But I'd just started this long journey. It would be a while before God's peace could truly rule in my heart. At least I was headed in the right direction.

During our next prayer time together, Ed suggested I write a letter to my dad. "Not to give to him, but so you can see and release the pain that lives in your heart."

I expressed my hurts in a page and a half of ink. My dad didn't want me. He didn't care about me. He criticized and ignored me. I was rejected and unloved. I had thought something was wrong with me because I caused him so much unhappiness, and I became ashamed of myself. I blamed my dad for my bad relationships and for all my insecurities.

In doing this exercise, I saw that I hadn't forgiven my dad.

Five years before, I'd been at a church service when the pastor had an altar call for those who needed to extend forgiveness to their fathers. I went forward, along with many others, and the pastor prayed for me that day. Through tears, I professed forgiveness. In writing this letter, I realized that unforgiveness can run deep and hide in the crevices of the heart. I clearly had more work to do. I asked God to help me truly forgive.

Though I talked to Hannah most evenings on the phone, I hadn't seen her for a week. I called Dawn and told her I wanted to see Hannah. She invited me to come over for dinner after work.

As I drove to Dawn's house that evening, I was more nervous than excited. Dawn greeted me at the door and told me that Hannah was playing in the family room with her cousins, Erika and Nicole. I took a deep breath and slowly walked toward the sound of laughter. The three girls were sitting on the floor playing a game. Hannah must have heard my footsteps because she quickly spun around.

"Mama!" She got up and raced toward me. I knelt down to receive the hug that was coming. I embraced her and smothered her cheek with kisses. She did the same to me.

"Are you having fun playing with the girls?" I asked as I fought back tears.

"Yeah," she replied.

I took her hand and led her back to the game so it could continue. I sat on the floor with the girls and talked with them while they finished.

Dinner was soon ready, so we took our places at the kitchen table. There we were, Dawn, her husband Rob, their kids, Hannah, and me. Dawn had prepared a chicken and pasta dish, along with vegetables and fresh fruit.

My niece, Nicole, offered to say grace. We closed our eyes and bowed our heads. She asked God to bless the food and then thanked Him that I came to visit. The awkwardness I felt quickly left as the food was passed around the table. The meal and time together was such a gift, but as usual my stomach soured, and I wasn't able to eat much.

After dinner Dawn suggested that her kids help clean up the kitchen, so Hannah and I could spend uninterrupted time together. It was good to be alone with my precious girl. We played games in the family room until Dawn's kids joined us.

At eight o'clock it was time for Hannah to go to bed. She said goodnight to everyone, and we went upstairs to get her settled in for the night. I chuckled when I saw that her cousin's bed had been taken over by her blankets and stuffed animals. I helped her get ready for bed, then she snuggled herself under her pile of blankets.

"I enjoyed being with you tonight," I told her with a big smile.

"Me too, Mama," she replied.

Choke her, a voice whispered.

Alarmed at the evil thought, I jumped up. "I have to go honey." Never before did I have thoughts of hurting my daughter.

As I headed for the door, Hannah asked, "When can I come home?"

"I don't know. Soon, I hope." I blew her a kiss.

I joined my sister in the kitchen, and we talked for a while. I told her that Ed and I had been praying and that God revealed that I hadn't truly forgiven our dad.

"I knew you hadn't forgiven him," she replied in a haughty tone.

Sensing our already strained relationship heading for more tension, I stood up to leave and said, "I'm tired. I should go."

She walked me to the foyer and handed me my coat. After I put it on, she wrapped her arms around me and held me tight. With a catch in her throat, she said, "I just want my sister back."

As I drove home, the devil's words against Hannah replayed in my mind. Nervously, I called Dawn on my cell phone. "Can you please make sure Hannah is safe in bed?"

"Uh, okay. Hang on a minute." After a period of silence she returned and said, "Hannah's just fine, safe in bed."

I could tell she was annoyed, but I needed reassurance that Hannah was all right. I needed to know that I had not harmed her.

I'd made arrangements with Dawn to bring Hannah home for the afternoon on Saturday. Hannah knew I was coming and she greeted me at the door, ready to go. We had a great time playing games together, and she was a welcome distraction from my constant anxiety. Shortly before dinner I sat her on my lap and said, "It's time to go back to Auntie Dawn's house."

"Please let me stay here," she pleaded. "I don't want to leave."

My heart broke and I whispered, "Mama's getting better, but I'm not ready for you to stay here all the time yet."

The five mile drive to my sister's felt like fifty. When we got to Dawn's house, she was waiting for us, and opened the door before we knocked. The three of us stood awkwardly in the entryway. I knelt down to say good-bye to Hannah. "Be good for Auntie Dawn," I said in between kisses. "Be strong for me. I love you sweetie."

"I don't want you to go," she bawled.

I pulled myself away from her, as I didn't want her to see me cry. "I'll call you tomorrow," I hollered as I walked toward my car.

I could hear her wailing, but by the time I turned around, the door was closing.

Dawn called me the next day. She explained that Hannah had fussed all night after I left. That made things more difficult on Dawn and her family.

"I'm sorry about that," I replied. "But we need to see each other."

"Well, I've decided that while she stays in my home, you are not allowed to visit her."

Angered by my sister's mandate and motivated to see Hannah, I made an appointment with a Christian psychiatrist and started anti-anxiety medications.

On the drive home after a busy work day, I began reminding myself of who God is and who I am. I began by saying, "God is faithful, God is merciful, God is my Father." Then it changed to, "God loves me, God is pleased with me." That progressed to, "My Daddy loves me, my Daddy is pleased with me, my Daddy accepts me."

As I spoke those words out loud in my car, I started bawling like a baby. For the first time in forty-two years, I could say I was loved and accepted—and not just by a human dad, but by God Himself. My heart felt light. I was elated about my relationship with God.

Wherever God is at work, so is the devil. He began to mutter insinuations to me. He suggested that since I had been wrong about

God's character, I could be wrong about other things pertaining to God as well. Because my beliefs about God had changed, he hinted that I should question my foundation.

Though my newfound truths about God were glorious, I found myself thrashing around in the devil's whirlpool of innuendos. I knew I needed a lifeboat. I asked Ed to pray with me. We asked God to reveal the truth about the foundation on which I stood. As we circled about our prayer room, God gave Ed a word of knowledge. "If Christ is your foundation, your faith can grow and change, but the foundation of your faith cannot change. Even though your view of God has been shaken, the foundation remains sturdy. As Hebrews 13:8 says, 'Jesus Christ is the same yesterday, today, and forever.'

"Psalm 62:6 says, 'He only is my rock and my salvation; He is my defense; I shall not be moved.' God your rock hasn't changed, but you feel insecure because your understanding of Him has changed."

If Christ is your foundation, your faith can grow and change, but the foundation of your faith cannot change.

"Yes, it's the attributes of God, the first person of the Trinity that I'm struggling to comprehend. My perceptions of Jesus and the Holy Spirit aren't affected. I still feel safe with them."

Ed suggested, "Since you're secure with Jesus, then answer the devil with, 'Jesus is my rock. He is my foundation and my defense, and I will not be moved!'"

I may not have had all the answers on how to relate to God as my Father, but I knew Jesus. He was my firm foundation.

A huge answer to prayer: only five days after starting medication, my anxiety was sufficiently controlled. The knot in my stomach relaxed, so I was able to eat more. Soon I felt physically stronger. More importantly, I felt safe enough to bring Hannah home.

When I called my sister to let her know I was ready to pick up Hannah from preschool the next day, she questioned whether or not I was truly up for the task. "I don't mind keeping her longer if you need me to," she said. "I'm concerned about her being safe with you. I think you should wait a little longer." After further discussion she reluctantly yielded to my decision and agreed to relinquish Hannah.

The next day I surprised Hannah when I poked my head in her classroom and asked her, "Are you ready to come home?" A smile spread across her face and she jumped up and down excitedly as she ran toward me. I knelt down and hugged her, stroking her silky black hair.

She chattered almost non-stop as we drove to our house. When we got there, she ran up the stairs and into her bedroom. She played with her toys as if they were long-lost friends. Later that night, after reading to her from her Bible and tucking her in, I realized she hadn't slept in her own bed for almost three weeks. It seemed like a life time.

Hannah's coming home so fast was an unexpected blessing. But soon afterward, I started hearing the words *I hate you.* The words weren't audible; they seemed internal, and as if they were coming from my chest. I was afraid these words were my feelings toward God. But that didn't make sense because I didn't hate God. Feeling uneasy, I called Ed and told him about this.

"It sounds like the devil is talking to you."

"I don't think so. The words are coming *from* me, not at me. And not *to* my mind, but *from* my chest."

That night I had a dream. I was angry at my dad for some reason and I swore at him. I was shocked by the profanity I used; I hadn't said those words in many years. Did I have some hidden anger toward my dad?

The *I hate you* voice continued over the next several days. I tried to ignore it, but each day it became louder and occurred more frequently. I could hardly concentrate at work.

I became so desperate to get rid of it that when I drove home from work one day, I decided to admit that maybe I still hated my dad, even though I didn't think I did. I started listing the reasons I used to hate him. Then I heard myself say, "I hated you so much I said I wouldn't go to your funeral if you died."

I gasped. I had completely buried the depth of my hatred for my dad.

I realized what had been going on. The *I hate you* voice was from a prisoner held captive in my heart from times past. He had been crying out to get noticed. I heard his cries, but I couldn't release him until I remembered the chains that bound him. He was gone now—and he took the hook in my heart with him.

I called Ed and told him what happened. "God is doing a work in your heart," he exclaimed. Did He have to do it while the devil attacked me?!

Ed and I decided we should meet to pray about this big event that just occurred. On the drive over, Ed kept hearing *Matthew 21:44*. After he arrived he looked it up and read it out loud. "'Whoever falls on this stone will be broken; but on whomever it falls, it will grind him to powder.' The stone in this verse refers to Jesus. When we ask

Jesus into our hearts, He becomes our Savior. He only becomes our Lord if we fall upon Him and become broken. Like salvation, this decision is voluntary. If we throw ourselves on the stone, we have to become humble and hold nothing back. Then our hearts break open and expose what needs to be removed."

When we ask Jesus into our hearts, He becomes our Savior. He only becomes our Lord if we fall upon Him and become broken.

"God wants me to fall on Him and have broken-hearted submission?" I asked.

"Yes. Only then can He remove the devil's weapons from your heart and pour in the fullness of His love."

I quietly prayed and thought about what that would look like.

Ed interrupted my thoughts with another verse. "First John 4:16 says, 'We have known and believed the love that God has for us. God is love, and he who abides in love abides in God and God in him.'"

Ed explained, "The love God has for us is in motion; it flows continually, like a river. It never becomes stagnant, but is always fresh and pure. We can't outrun His love. Nor can we hide from it. I see an image of a cup filled with water from a river. This is a picture of God in us. When that full-to-the-rim cup is dropped back into the river of love, we are in Him. The same time we're in God, God is in us, continuously filling us with His sweet, flowing love.

"I sense a change in the environment. A deep, tender reverence has come into the room. It's solemn, like when you enter the home of a friend whose child is gravely ill." Ed looked at me and said, "There's a wound in your heart. It's not deadly, but it is destructive."

A vision came to my mind. I was sitting on God's lap. I wanted Him to hold me. Instead, I pounded on His chest with my tightly clenched fists. Was I angry at God because He didn't rescue me when I was abused?

Ed said, "The solemn reverence I feel is God's compassion. God's daughter, the King's daughter, has been deeply wounded. God wants you to know that He protected you and did everything He could to help you—but He couldn't override your dad's free will. However, as your dad inflicted wounds, God was with you, holding flowers and balloons for His hurting little girl."

Authority in Christ

Nevertheless do not rejoice in this, that the spirits are subject to you, but rather rejoice because your names are written in heaven.
—*Luke 10:20*

IT HAD BEEN A MONTH since the night of the crisis occurred. The medication had brought my anxiety level down so that I could concentrate. I started to read my Bible again. As I read I heard, *I don't believe that* or *That's not true*. I assumed these thoughts were mine and was afraid I didn't believe God's Word anymore.

When I looked at certain symbols of my faith, like pictures of Jesus or my cross necklace, I heard bad thoughts about Jesus or God. And during my pastor's sermons, I heard thoughts of disbelief about what he was saying. Sometimes these thoughts were louder than the pastor's words! I also heard things such as, *You should leave the church and never come back*. Every time I tried to read God's Word or focus on God, I was blasted with negative thoughts.

Naturally, the thoughts overwhelmed me, so I stopped reading my Bible and going to church—two things I needed most at this time. The thoughts intensified by encompassing even non-spiritual activities and it became a full-time job trying to shut them out of my mind. I was exhausted by the mental exertion and started getting headaches. I wanted to stab my head with an ice pick, just to get the thoughts out. As waves of anxiety flooded back in, I repeatedly asked myself, *What is wrong with me?*

I told Ed what was happening, and we went to God for help.

As we prayed, revelation knowledge came to Ed. "You should change your question from 'What is wrong with me?' to 'What is happening to me?' because those thoughts aren't yours. Satan has assigned a harassing spirit to deter you."

Ed stopped walking and stared at the floor. After a minute or two he said, "Denise, come here."

I walked over and stood in front of him. "Do whatever you have to do, just get it off me."

He boldly commanded, "In the name of Jesus Christ whose I am and whom I serve, you harassing spirit depart from her now! Go!"

I looked at my picture of Jesus. Silence. "The spirit is gone!" I exclaimed. I was relieved, but disturbed.

Ed said, "That's good, but I'm sensing we're not done with this battle quite yet. Were you involved with someone when you worked at the state hospital?"

I worked as a nurse practitioner at the state psychiatric hospital, but hadn't been there in over a year. As I thought about my time there, I recalled a specific patient. "There was a woman I remember quite well who said she was a witch. I only had contact with her once, but I remember feeling very uneasy as I conducted my routine examine."

"I don't know if that witch put a spell on you, but I do know that there is still a demonic assignment against you."

As we started our circular prayer walk again, Ed declared, "In the name of Jesus, I break any spells or commands that the wicked servants of Satan have cast over you. I break those assignments, and they cannot come on you anymore." Then Ed proclaimed scriptures over me. "He who is in you is greater than he who is in the world" (1 John 4:4) and "No evil shall befall you, nor shall any plague come near your dwelling" (Ps. 91:10).

Ed pulled out a small bottle of anointing oil from his pocket. "The Holy Spirit is leading me to wipe this on the doors and windows of your house."

"Whatever it takes, Ed." I followed him into every room, making sure he didn't miss a single entry point, including the garage door.

We felt we had great victory over that harassing spirit. I was a little freaked out that an evil being had been attached to me, but I didn't have much time to process the experience. Within a few days, I was attacked again. This time I started hearing *I reject Jesus* throughout the day. I ordered the evil spirits to leave me alone. They didn't listen. Would this battle ever be over?

I asked Ed to come over to pray about this. After a few minutes of petitioning God, Ed said, "You don't know how to operate in the authority of Christ. Matthew 10:16 says, 'Behold, I send you out as sheep in the midst of wolves. Therefore be wise as serpents and harmless as doves.' We are prey in a world full of predators and to survive, we need to be wise as serpents. A serpent knows how to hide, but it also knows how to fight."

"I'm gaining knowledge of the enemy's tactics, but that doesn't help much if I'm ignorant of my authority or incompetent in exercising it."

"Don't feel bad," Ed said. "Most other Christians don't get it either. I don't have special abilities. I used the name of Jesus and exercised the authority God has given me. I was drawing from the power of God Almighty. And that power is available to you too!"

I realized that this training was crucial: Satan was out to destroy me, and I didn't know how to use my defenses.

Ed took a drink of water and then continued, "These attacks keep coming because you're not wearing the symbol of God's authority, which I envision as the badge of Christ. And you can't put it on until all the unforgiveness is out of your heart. Don't worry, your ability to wear His badge will come—as you allow God to purify you.

"Furthermore, to back up the badge, God has equipped you with a sword—the sword of the Spirit, which is the Word of God. The sword is the power behind the badge. To use it effectively, the Word of God has to be firmly fixed in your heart and spoken boldly."

I told Ed that I didn't think I had that part of God's Word settled in my heart. It was hard for me to believe that God gave *me* authority and power over the devil (Luke 10:19). I wondered how I could speak scripture boldly if I lacked the confidence that the power of God resided in me.

Ed continued, "God just gave me an illustration that might help change your perspective. Imagine that as you're walking to your car, you see the door open and broken glass all around. If a child is standing there with a rock in his hand, you would no doubt grab him and call the police. That's how you need to see the devil, as a weak and powerless six-year-old. You've mistakenly envisioned him as strong and powerful, like a well-trained boxer. So rather than restrain him, you let him take whatever he wants."

It was sinking in. The devil is not a mighty boxer. He has the power of a small child plus a really big mouth! First Peter 5:8 says, "Be sober, be vigilant; because your adversary the devil walks about like a roaring lion, seeking whom he may devour." The devil walks around *like* a roaring lion, but he is not a lion. The real Lion is from the tribe of Judah, and He was starting to roar in me!

> *The devil is not a mighty boxer. He has the power of a small child plus a really big mouth!*

Learning to use the sword, the Word of God, effectively, required practice. Over the next few days, I spoke scriptures on authority as often as I could. I boldly commanded spirits by saying, "In the name of Jesus get away from me!" It seemed that sometimes they obeyed and sometimes they didn't. When the devil talked to me, I didn't engage with him but spoke out loud, "It is written . . ." I also continued to proclaim who God is and who I am in Christ.

I endeavored to be strong, but the devil was persistent in fighting these daily battles with me. In the depths of my soul, I was flat on my back. The only good thing about this low place I found myself in was that my face was pointed in the right direction: looking up toward God.

Here my attitude changed. I cared that the devil was trying to kill me, but I no longer cared if I lived life my way. I decided that *I* was done. *I* was done being in charge of my life. *I* was done trying to do things in my own strength. These battles needed to end, and I was willing to do whatever I had to do.

Jesus told His disciples in Matthew 16:24, "If anyone desires to come after Me, let him deny himself, and take up his cross, and follow Me." In this dark place, I surrendered myself and my agenda to Jesus. I was ready to pick up my cross and follow Him. I would go wherever He led me and would do whatever He told me to do—no matter the cost. I had no idea where God would take me, but it didn't matter anymore. We were holding hands now.

In the past I had resisted letting go of my agenda because I trusted myself. But Proverb 3:5 says, "Trust in the LORD with all your heart and lean not on your own understanding." God desired that I experience this humbling place of dying to self. I would learn to trust Him here, and I would know it was Him who brought me out. My new motto became, "Not my will but yours, Lord."

I had been under tremendous demonic attack, so I didn't have much joy left. I started to feel sorry for myself. I thought I had been a big disappointment to God. I was mad at myself for being in this situation. Once again, I met with Ed to pray.

As I walked and prayed, Ed searched for the verse God was directing him to. He said, "Psalm 118:24 says, 'This is the day the Lord has made; we will rejoice and be glad in it.' If you want to feel sorry for yourself, that's your choice. But you can choose to have joy instead of sorrow—no matter how bad your life is.

"Nehemiah 8:10 says, 'For the joy of the Lord is your strength.' Without joy you won't have strength, so you can't afford to listen to the enemy tell you how miserable you should feel. He wants to steal your joy so you won't have the wherewithal to keep fighting the good fight. If you have the joy of the Lord, you'll have the strength to hold up your shield of faith—the one that quenches the devil's fiery darts" (Eph. 6:16).

I asked Ed how I could get joy in the midst of my sadness. He reminded me to express my love to God with words of praise. He said I should focus on God's promises and remind myself of how much God loved me, how great God was, and the many things He had already done for me. This would produce great joy, and this joy would carry with it great strength.

A couple of days later I visited Ed's church. After the service seven of us gathered together to pray. A young woman in the group told us that the Lord awakened her that morning with the instruction to *resist the devil.*

Seeking clarification or a word from the Lord, we began praying in tongues. In the midst of our prayers, Ed hollered, "There's a fight with demons in this room."

An older woman approached me. "Are you the one fighting demons?" she asked.

I nodded my head.

She put her hands on my shoulders and prayed. I felt the power of God come upon me. I was overcome and slumped to the floor. As I lay there, two women sang over me and prayed that I would have rest and rebuilding. As they did that, Ed walked around the room calling out, "See the will of the Lord" over and over.

After I got up, the young woman said to me, "I saw a creature come off you. It looked doglike or monkeylike and it went and crouched in the corner." Then God gave her a word of knowledge: "This demon was a spirit of unworthiness—and it has a right to stalk you."

Bothered by what that woman disclosed, Ed and I got together to pray a few days later. We asked God to shed His light in the darkness and expose the lies of unworthiness.

Words of knowledge came through Ed. "The devil used your childhood experiences to place corrupt building blocks in your heart. He firmly cemented them into place, laying a foundation of wrong ideas about your self-worth. Over the years you accepted them as truth. These building blocks, these lies of the devil, are keeping you from the freedoms found in Christ. Believing that you're unworthy allows that demon to continue tracking you."

Ed asked me to bring up Hebrews 4:12 on my computer. It reads, "For the word of God is living and powerful and sharper than any two-edged sword, piercing even to the division of soul and spirit, and of joints and marrow, and is a discerner of the thoughts and intents of the heart."

You will also come to know God as your deliverer, not from the sins you've committed, but from the sins committed against you.

Ed said, "God will continue using His Word to remove the deceptions from your heart. The truth will set you free so you can be the woman you're meant to be."

"But a lot of my childhood is hidden away," I protested. "I don't know if I'll be able to remember those things." Ed reminded me that nothing is beyond the power of the Holy Spirit, not even the enemy's concealed weapons.

Then Ed prophesied, "The time has come for God to shine His holy light on those defective building blocks. He will not only show you the false beliefs and opinions you have about yourself, but He will also perform open-heart surgery and remove them. You will also come to know God as your deliverer, not from the sins you've committed, but from the sins committed against you."

A few nights later as I cooked dinner, I sensed a force behind me. The spirit starting exerting pressure on the back of my head; it was trying to push its way in. I resisted it, but it was too strong and it penetrated my mind. My thoughts became inundated with swear words, aimed at God and others. I mustered up the authority I knew I had in Christ and in His name I commanded the spirit to leave. After wrestling with it for the better part of a week, I asked Ed if he would pray with me about it.

We came to God with the question: why does this weapon that's formed against me seem to be prospering? Revelation came through Ed. "There's an entrance, a door of opportunity for the enemy to come through. The door is small, like a mouse hole chewed in a baseboard, but it's an opening nonetheless. The devil continually comes in because he can; an avenue of approach is accessible."

I asked God to show us the avenue and what we could do to fix the hole!

After a few minutes of praying, Ed stopped and looked at me. "This mouse hole is a stronghold—one of many. These strongholds are unresolved wounds and lies in your heart that the devil planted long ago. He's using them against you now. They work like a failsafe device. In the event that you ever turned to Christ for salvation, the devil could still have access to you. One of the lies has to do with your self-perception. As a little girl, your heart cried out for your daddy's love, but since he refused to give it, you believe you're unworthy of love—even God's love."

Feeling a little discouraged over this issue that I thought I had addressed, I said, "I know the Bible says Jesus has made me worthy. God has even declared His acceptance and love for me recently!"

Ed explained that I could only mentally assent to those things because the rejected wounded girl I became was still chained in my heart. I wanted God's love, and yet I was rejecting it. In the dark secret places of my heart, I didn't truly believe God could love me. The evidence of my unworthiness prohibited me from changing my self-perception and made me incapable of receiving God's love.

"How can I change my self-portrait? How can I stop seeing myself as unworthy of love once and for all, and accept God's love?" I asked.

Ed challenged me by asking if God could lie about His love for me.

"Of course God cannot lie," I replied.

"So you have a choice to make. You can either believe the devil's lies that you're unworthy of love, or you can believe that God loves you more than you can understand."

I didn't want to reject God's love, so in my heart I decided that I was lovable and God truly did love me.

I didn't want to reject God's love, so in my heart I decided that I was lovable and God truly did love me. That simple heart change put a dent in the chain that bound the girl suffering inside of me. I was making progress. And my loving heavenly Father would not give up on me. He would gently break the chain—making one dent at a time. One day I would be set free.

The swearing and hearing *I reject Jesus* continued. Ed and I talked about it with a woman from his church. I remarked that at least I couldn't be possessed by a demon. She disagreed and then told us her story.

"When I came to the Cross my sins were forgiven, but unbeknown to me, I had a spirit of addiction living inside. For ten years I was filled with the Holy Spirit and used by God, but I was a slave to the demon and couldn't stop using cocaine."

I looked at Ed somewhat skeptically.

She went on. "I knew an elderly man who had spiritual authority and asked him to deliver me. As he spoke to the spirit, I became aware of something looking out from my eyes. Feelings of hatred toward this man welled up inside me—those feelings belonged to the demon. Experienced in these matters, he saw the spirit looking at him and prayed more fervently. The demon came out, and my addiction was gone. As the demon left, it felt as if someone was pulling a sheet out of my body."

I believed her testimony, and it rang true in Ed's spirit. It did, however, go against what Ed had learned in Bible college—that you can't be filled with the Holy Spirit and possessed by demons at the same time. He needed time to process this.

This assault against me was taking its toll. There had been promptings and suggestions of suicide, anxiety-provoking lies that I was Hell bound, and harassing evil spirits. But I took comfort in the fact that I had not been defeated. God had given me victory after victory.

Nevertheless, after two long months of battle, I was tired of the daily fight. I felt like a frayed rope; God and Satan were playing tug of war with my spirit, both desperate to have me. I asked Ed if we could pray.

Ed shared Galatians 4:7. "Therefore you are no longer a slave but a son, and if a son, then an heir of God through Christ." Ed continued, "Denise, we are not only God's adopted heirs through Christ as this verse says, but as Romans 8:17 tells us, we are also joint heirs with Christ. This means we have the same authority over the devil and his works that Jesus does! As joint heirs, demons have to obey us. As foul and nasty as they are, they cannot violate God's Word when it's spoken in Christ's authority."

> We are also joint heirs with Christ. This means we have the same authority over the devil and his works that Jesus does!

Even though Ed was talking to me, I sensed that God was speaking more to Ed. I didn't respond to him, I just began walking and praying. Ed did the same until another verse came to him and he spoke Matthew 11:12. "'And from the days of John the Baptist until now, the kingdom of heaven suffers violence, and the violent take it by force.' We have to take the kingdom of Heaven by force because demons stand in our way. We have to forcefully assert the power and authority God gave us when we became joint heirs with Christ."

The perplexed look on my face prompted Ed to continue. "When you became a daughter of the King, He gave you a robe of righteousness, a crown, and a scepter. He expects you to walk as a princess in authority. You are to carry yourself with confidence and use your most commanding voice. When you pray in tongues, do so in an authoritative manner, like a Monarch speaking to her subjects. Be bold in the face of the enemy, knowing that God, not the devil, is in charge of your life."

Ed began walking faster and he sounded agitated. "We can't walk in God's authority with only a defensive strategy. An offensive approach is required, but it won't be successful through the use of power only. Zechariah 4:6 says, 'Not by might nor by power, but by My Spirit, says the LORD of hosts.' We have to submit not only to God and Jesus, but to the Holy Spirit as well."

Ed quit walking and looked at me. "I've never done this before, but I'm going to try casting a demon out of you. I don't need to lay hands on you or anoint you with oil; I just want you to be in agreement with me."

I agreed.

Ed stood in front of me and forcefully prayed, "Because of Jesus Christ whose I am and whom I serve, you demon, you come out of her. You lying, swearing, cursing demon, come out now! In the name and power of Jesus Christ, you must come out. Don't resist and don't delay. Just get out!"

My eyelids began to flutter like moth wings. I wasn't in pain, but I was distraught. I exclaimed, "Something's wrong with my eyes! I can't see!"

Ed was unmoved by my condition and sat me down on the floor. He continued, "You are not authorized to be in there. You cannot resist the Word of God or the power of God, and you cannot violate the command. You cannot have her, she belongs to God Almighty. She will never be yours, her heart is knit with God's heart and God's heart is knit with hers. She is washed in the blood of Christ and you have no authority over her. You are not welcome, you cannot come back, and you have no power to return. You can't stay in this house either. Get out of this house. So be it by the Word of God."

As Ed exercised his authority in Christ, my ears burned hot and I felt something inside me travel upward from my abdomen through my chest and come out of my mouth like a puff of air or smoke.

When Ed finished his command, he praised God for providing us with His power. Then he said to me, "The kingdom of Heaven is here on earth and the power of God is available. Jesus said in John 14:12, 'Most assuredly, I say to you, he who believes in Me, the works that I do he will do also; and greater works than these he will do, because I go to My Father.' I believe we've experienced that today."

I was disturbed that I'd had an evil spirit inside me, yet I couldn't deny what happened. I didn't know what kind of spirit it was as I didn't have an addiction like the lady I met at Ed's church. I hoped the swearing in my head would go away with the demon, but it was still there. Even so, I knew we were making progress, so I asked Ed to pray with me about this again.

As we entered our prayer room, Ed and I talked about demons. He said he studied the topic and found some reputable sources that conclude that people can have demons in them even after being saved and filled with the Holy Spirit. There are two distinct facets of demon possession, one in which a demon takes over a person entirely—spirit, soul, and body, and one in which a demon lives in a person, yet the person is not completely possessed by it. Ed said, "You did have a demon in you, but you weren't completely possessed by it because it didn't control you."

As we began to pray, Ed told me, "I hear the word *resistance* in my spirit. Let's pray louder and more forcefully."

We raised our voice levels, made our tones demanding, and quickened our strides. After a few minutes, Ed stood in front of me and boldly commanded, "Come out of her now you lying, swearing spirit, you cannot resist, you cannot hide. You cannot stay, and you cannot come back!"

Nothing happened.

The spirit told Ed that his kind would only come out with much prayer and fasting. Ed circled around me and rebuked the spirit, "That's not true. You WILL come out at the command of the Word of God."

Ed put his hand on my forehead and said, "You're burning hot!" He demanded that the spirit leave my body, in the name of Jesus. All of a sudden my lungs felt irritated, and I started coughing. In a short while the cough was gone. The swearing was not.

Again Ed commanded, "No, no, no, you're not staying here. You're beat. You are defeated. You will not resist this. You cannot." Ed touched my forehead again and remarked that it was still on fire.

Ed demanded, "You come out of her head now, you swearing demon, you harassing spirit. Come out right now. You have to come out in Jesus name. You cannot have the victory; you have been defeated. You must exit as you have no authority. You have no lease, no promise to stay. There is a new resident and it is the Holy Spirit! Jesus gave His disciples power over all the works of the enemy. I am His disciple, so in the name of Jesus, because of the name of Jesus, you are hereby defeated!"

As Ed prayed my legs became weak, and I sank to the floor. I felt shaky. Unfortunately, I couldn't tell if a spirit had left. After Ed helped me up, we prayed again. During our prayer, Ed got the impression that maybe this attack was due to some confession I made long ago.

Ed asked the Lord to reveal any permission slips or contracts I may have signed that violated His Word.

The words, *a vow, a vow, a vow,* echoed in Ed's spirit. Then revelation knowledge flowed from Ed. "There were vows made at church when you were a girl. You need to revisit those vows and break their bonds. This will be as binding as the original vows were."

I wasn't sure what they were at the moment, but I told Ed that I had an inkling it had to do with my first communion or confirmation.

Ed said, "Repeat after me: I disavow the teachings of my childhood church and any verbal or written commitments I made to the church, to Mary, and to the Pope."

I didn't remember making vows *per se*, so it felt awkward. But I did it sincerely with the authority of Christ in me. When I finished, Ed recommended that I affirm my allegiance to God, Jesus, and the Holy Spirit. Without hesitation, I said, "I pledge myself, my heart, and my life to God. I declare that I will live for Him alone. I pledge myself to Jesus, and I proclaim Him as my Savior, Healer, Master, and King. I vow to always follow Him. I acknowledge that the Holy Spirit lives inside me. I give Him permission to have control over me, to teach me, to reveal things to me, and to transform me."

Ed asked me if I had any relics from my childhood church, things that I held dear or treasured.

I told him I had several items. I had the rosary from my first communion, a necklace with a picture of Jesus enclosed in crystal, a picture of Jesus I won when I was five, and a crucifix my mom gave me. "I haven't wanted these things for years, but I can't throw them away either. I feel as if I would be throwing Jesus in the garbage."

Ed quoted Exodus 20:25. "And if you make Me an altar of stone, you shall not build it of hewn stone; for if you use your tool on it, you have profaned it." Ed explained that human hands made the rosary, necklace, picture, and crucifix, so they could not be holy. Ed said, "Their only significance is the value you've attached to them. In this case, they have a negative value—they're remnants of false beliefs."

I ran upstairs and rummaged through my house for those man-made items. I promptly threw them—and the deceptions that came with them—away.

Killing the Old Man

My dishonor is continually before me,
and the shame of my face has covered me.
—Psalm 44:15

FOR THREE MONTHS my spirit had been trained and exercised in warfare, and my spiritual perception was becoming strong. My life was so immersed in spiritual matters that I had trouble knowing what reality was anymore. I had a dual life. By day I went to work or cared for Hannah, and by night I battled demons and God revealed secrets and mysteries.

I still fought the swearing and a barrage of negative thoughts about God. Only now, my spirit was aware of them approaching, and I could block the thoughts before they entered my mind. Eventually, the swearing stopped and the unwanted thoughts diminished. Unfortunately, when the devil's tactics stop working, he switches to something else.

Ed and I were talking one day and I remembered that as I slept the night before, God spoke *hindrance* to my spirit. Ed asked me, "What is a hindrance and what does it do?"

I told him that it prevents something.

"And it can be invisible," Ed added. "You have a hindrance assigned to you, and Satan is behind it. I also see that God has not forbidden it, and therefore He likely won't remove it."

As we prayed together, Ed said, "I sense the hindrance. A demon is in our way. To overcome his resistance and move him, we have to use the power of the Holy Spirit."

We waged war on the demon by being audacious and by aggressively praying in tongues. Then to my surprise, Ed started laughing. He exclaimed, "He's gone! We have the victory! Did you feel that?"

I said, "I don't know what you experienced, but I felt the floor rise up to meet my feet." Ed said the height of the ceiling seemed to have changed. Before, it felt as if the room had a five-foot ceiling and we couldn't stand up straight. Now the ceiling seemed ten feet high and there was plenty of room to stand tall. We had been raised up from oppression—the floor even moved! The environment felt righteous and holy.

Ed explained, "The hindrance was not moved just by praying in tongues. Our anger at the devil trying to stop you caused righteous indignation to rise up within us. Our godly wrath came against him through prayer and pushed him out of the way, thereby defeating the hindrance."

Ed helped me understand that since I was the one hindered, I was responsible for overcoming it. God could have intervened, but He expected me, with Ed's help, to push through it rather than side step it or ask Him to remove it for me. Now that the demon was gone, I could move toward whatever had been hindered.

About a week later, I had a dream that my sister and her family were moving out of state. The dream really bothered me, so I called my sister, Dawn, and asked her about it. She said it was a possibility they were considering. The idea of them leaving me caused a great deal of anxiety. I had trouble sleeping too. I asked Ed if he would pray with me about my sister's potential move.

Ed was able to come over that same day, so we spent some time petitioning the Lord. Ed paused and said to me, "God has revealed to me that throughout your childhood, you looked to your sister to tell you who you should be. That caused you to idolize her."

I knew Ed was speaking the truth. Even as an adult, I admired my sister and relied on her to define me. I wore clothes that she picked out for me and even furnished parts of my home according to her taste. I tried hard to please my sister and earn her love—just like I had done with my dad. I knew I shouldn't need my sister's approval, and I wanted my lifelong dependence on her opinions to end. But I didn't know how to take her off the pedestal.

I expressed my feelings to Ed, and he helped me understand. "You still view yourself as subordinate to your sister because the picture of who you are in Christ is not fully developed—and can't be if you continue to look to Dawn for your identity. God doesn't want you subservient to her or to anyone on this earth. Jesus is your only authority, your only master."

Ed also relayed that God wanted me to develop a fresh, new relationship with my sister, one in which we were equals.

The knowledge God gave me this day, combined with my desire to end the reliance on my sister, caused my dependence on Dawn to instantly die. As I envisioned my idol shattering and crashing to the ground, relief flooded my body. I knew if my sister moved I would be okay, and more importantly, I finally felt liberated from a lifetime of trying to measure up. I told Ed, "I resolve not to let anyone, except God, influence me." The Bible says to have no other gods—and that included my sister.

> *I resolve not to let anyone, except God, influence me.*

For quite a while I blocked negative thoughts and commanded evil spirits to flee. I also learned some new things along the way. Sometimes when I told the spirits to go, they didn't listen unless I specifically addressed them as a harassing spirit. Also, I got tired of listening to demons refute what I said to God. To put an end to that, I started talking internally to God. For example, I silently told God, "Yes Lord, I will follow you," but I heard, "No Lord, I won't," rise up inside me. Talking to God like this did not solve my problem, and I began to suspect that I was battling something within.

For the most part my anxiety was controlled. I had only seen the psychiatrist twice; he said he didn't need to see me anymore and told me I could stop the anxiety medication after six months. I intended to follow his advice, but quit taking the medicine ahead of schedule because it made my head feel like it was in the clouds. I made the right choice because my head cleared up when I stopped the medication. I would have to deal with anxiety symptoms if they returned.

My relationship with my parents was back to normal, but my sister and I weren't talking much. She knew I was praying often with Ed, and since I wasn't confiding in her, she felt I was being secretive. I just didn't know how to explain to her what was happening.

Hannah was happy and seemed to enjoy when Ed came over to pray. He brought a sense of calm to the home, and besides, she got to do what she pleased upstairs.

My friendship with Ed was evolving. Because of the large age gap, there was no romance of any kind. However, issues had come out in our prayer sessions that made me feel vulnerable. They were things I would have chosen to keep to myself if I could, but without Ed, I would not have made so much progress. He saw me hit rock bottom and yet walked alongside me as I climbed out of the pit. I had never known such a devoted friend before Ed. It was a special friendship, and I was so thankful for it.

I continued to seek God alone in prayer and I tried to develop an intimate relationship with Him. My prayers progressed from, "My Daddy loves me and is pleased with me" to "I love my Daddy." I had never said those words before, not to my heavenly Father and certainly not to my earthly dad. It brought much joy to my heart.

Five months had passed since the night of the crisis, and I finally felt like I had returned to some sense of normalcy. I started helping Ed in his church. I cleaned the facility and bought the needed supplies. At last I felt I could offer something to society again.

One night I had Ed over for dinner, and once again, words of knowledge came through my friend. He said, "God is using our times of prayer to remove impurities from your heart—you're in the

Refiner's fire. The heat of God's holy fire is burning the ungodly beliefs and their habits out of your heart. God will repeatedly put you in His fire until all the impurities are gone. Embrace the process. If God finishes His work, your heart will be beautiful and pure; useable by the Refiner."

He continued, "Some of the attacks you've experienced were the devil's attempts to hinder you from going through God's fire. God wants to encourage you to continue with the fight and see it through. Psalm 30:5 says, 'Weeping may endure for a night, but joy comes in the morning.' You're weary of Satan's assaults, and the Refiner's fire is painful, but there will be great joy if you see it through."

During these battles, I said no to the devil and yes to God. I said yes as I sent Hannah to be with my sister for a time. I said yes to God even when it was hard just to stay alive. I called on God for help through my tears and anguish. That's exactly what God wanted.

Ed said, "As you've pressed through the hardships and passed through the fire, change has occurred on two levels. First, the onslaughts have turned you into a prayer warrior. When this battle began, you limped when we prayed; it was symbolic of being spiritually wounded. Now the limp is gone and you walk boldly. Also, there have been times when my spirit has been drawn to your right hand. To the natural eye it may look as if your hand makes insignificant gestures, but these movements are a spiritual tool that God has given you and they perform warfare activity." Ed went on to explain that a second level of change was occurring in my heart and spirit. Every time God delivered me from the schemes of the enemy, my faith and trust in Him increased.

I agreed, "Yes, and each truth He's revealed about me or my past has lightened the load that was weighing on my heart."

"He's cleaning the slate, so to speak, so you can develop an unadulterated relationship with Him. This process is also causing the language barrier between your mind and spirit to break down. Your mind is agreeing with and submitting to your spirit to a greater extent now, and since your spirit is already in submission to God, you're being led by the Holy Spirit more."

Ed sensed that God was happy with my progress. God was slowly changing me from the wounded soldier to the aggressive, fully-armored watchman on the wall. His righteous fire was burning the dross from my heart.

I was willing to continue to go through the Refiner's fire, but my frustration grew over the negative thoughts about God that kept creeping back into my mind. Through this, the enemy tried to subtly convince me that God was not carrying me through this after all. He wanted me to believe that God was not protecting me. I couldn't perceive the devil's lies, but I noticed my heart began to feel broken. I asked Ed to pray with me.

God's wisdom flowed through Ed during our next prayer session. "We have three parts that try to lead us: our spirit, our heart, and our mind. Some would argue the body as well. They all want to be in charge, any of them can dominate, and they certainly influence each other. The mind is the part that makes decisions though, after it gathers information from the spirit, heart, and the other senses."

Ed went on, "There are only two possible states of our spirit: alive to God or dead to God. But the heart is much more complex. It can go countless steps on a continuum and become either closer to God or farther from God, as it's easily moved by the ebb and flow of our emotions. Satan can't change the state of our spirits, but he can work double time to deceive our hearts into changing its location.

"When Satan pulled you away from God, your spirit was still alive to God, but your heart had moved away from Him. Satan planned then, and now, to deceive your heart and use it to convince your mind to lead your spirit away from God. This would result in your spiritual death. Proverb 15:13 says, 'A merry heart makes a cheerful countenance, but by sorrow of the heart, the spirit is broken.'"

Rather than follow my heart, my mind decided to run to God—after He gave me a wake-up call. Satan didn't succeed with the indirect route through my heart, so he changed his course and directly attacked my mind with lies of God's rejection. That sent me into a crisis. When that plan ultimately failed, he switched tactics and went for my heart again.

I told Ed, "Now Satan is gently pressing the tip of his knife into my heart. I didn't recognize that he was the one holding the knife." Satan had repeatedly whispered, *It's painful to belong to God*, and I slowly accepted the thought that it was harmful for me to be a Christian. I began to ask God why He continued to let the devil attack me. In my mind I knew God was faithful, but my heart felt the sadness of a jilted lover, a betrayed spouse. "I thought I had to defend my heart from harm—harm that came from the One who was supposed to love me," I said sadly.

Ed explained a harsh truth. "Satan made it appear as if God was the cause of your pain. His goal is always the same; to move you away from God so you renounce Christ and your spirit becomes dead to God."

I raised my hands and said, "Lord, please forgive me for blaming you." I looked at Ed in frustration and said, "Why am I still vulnerable to the devil's tricks?"

After a time of prayer, Ed said, "The enemy invades your heart because there's an open gate. You still feel unworthy to be God's daughter. To overcome this deep-seated lie, it's vital for you to come to terms with the fact that when you accepted Christ, you became *fully* worthy because His sacrifice made you *fully* righteous. Second Corinthians 5:21 says, 'For He made Him who knew no sin to be sin for us, that we might become the righteousness of God in Him.' Are you going to believe God and His Word?"

I knew God couldn't lie and His Word was true. I was worthy— whether I felt like it or not. As I pondered this, I realized that I didn't feel guilty about the things I'd done, the unworthiness resulted from who I thought I was. My mind believed I'd been made righteous, but my heart couldn't accept that I was worthy. As Prov- erb 23:7 says, "For as he thinks in his heart, so is he."

God revealed to Ed that my righteousness wasn't settled in my heart, so though I stood on the foundation of Christ, I saw myself on my old foundation of unwor- thiness. Ed explained, "To wholeheartedly believe your righteousness and see yourself on the new foundation, it's essential to understand that your self-portrait is still wrong. When Jesus became your Savior, you were set on the new foundation of Christ. The old foundation ceases to exist because Jesus destroyed it. Second Corinthians 5:17 says, 'Therefore, if anyone is in Christ, he is a new creation; old things have passed away; behold, all things have become new.' On your new foundation of Christ, you're a different person: YOU ARE WOR- THY."

I was worthy— whether I felt like it or not.

I already believed Jesus redeemed me and God put me on the new foundation of Christ. Now I realized that since God had moved me, it was impossible to be the old worthless me who used to stand on the old foundation. I *had* to stand on the new foundation. According to Acts 17:28 that is where I live and move and have my being.

I asked Ed, "What do I need to do from here?"

"Did you hear that? You said, *from here*, which means you've finally accepted the new foundation. Your feet are securely planted on the firm foundation of Christ and you no longer see yourself on the shaky ground of unworthiness!"

As our prayer time ended, I noticed my heart didn't feel sad anymore. As Jesus proclaimed, "You shall know the truth, and the truth shall make you free" (John 8:32). Sometimes freedom came quickly; when the devil's lies were revealed, the hurt in my heart just disappeared. The beauty of this verse is that it applies not only to spiritual truths, but also to every area of life.

God made another dent in the chain that bound the suffering girl in my heart.

The "old me" is referred to in Romans 6:6. It says, "Knowing this, that our old man was crucified with Him, that the body of sin might be done away with, that we should no longer be slaves of sin." Though I was no longer that old man blatantly sinning against God, I still maintained some of his beliefs. Perhaps that's why we need to put off the old man and his former conduct (Eph. 4:22). The old man, the part of me whose thoughts were distorted and who held on to deep-rooted lies, had to die. He had been trained by the enemy.

Most of my life, the devil told me lies about myself; I was unlovable and unworthy—ugly inside. I believed his lies and adopted them as my own because I saw credible evidence. But my opinions of me weren't accurate. I needed to revise my self-portrait. My mind and heart had to let my born-again spirit change them. Then I could believe what God said about me instead of the false descriptions I had come to believe about myself.

Within myself, I had a life and death struggle. Either the old man or the new creation had to go; they couldn't co-exist. Which life would I rather live? *I choose God*, I told myself, but inside me a very real fight continued over the ownership of my life.

Either the old man or the new creation had to go; they couldn't co-exist.

Satan had trained me to defend my unrighteous position at all costs. But the hold the devil had on me had been overcome by the blood of Christ and my confession of Him. Now Jesus was teaching me how to kill the old man.

Though life was relatively peaceful, God's presence seemed distant. Furthermore, I was feeling uncertain about how to approach God. I told Ed my concerns, and we took them to God in prayer. During that time, God gave Ed a word of wisdom. "You have difficulty going to God because you have a different relationship with Him now than you did when this attack began. At first you intensely pursued God, now you're walking with Him. The way you enter into His presence has to change. Rather than coming in fear, looking to be rescued, you need to come with joy and thankfulness. God seems far off because He's ahead of you, calling you toward Him. He's saying, 'Follow Me, follow Me, we have a ways to walk together yet.' The more you follow Him, the quieter He becomes. He can speak more softly because your spirit is becoming trained to hear His voice."

I was glad to hear that nothing was terribly wrong. Ed told me that he sensed that God was about to pull me into something deeper.

God wanted even more from me. By God's grace I was still in His kingdom, but there was more to do. More steps, more lessons, more tests. It was like I'd finished grade school and was ready for junior high. But the classes would get harder, so I'd need to study more and work on my skills.

"I don't want things to get harder," I said.

"God thinks you're ready," Ed replied.

I attended Ed's church again, and after the service he prayed for some of the members. When it was my turn, he just stood in front of me. "Um, uh, I don't know what to say. I feel like the Holy Spirit is preventing me from praying for you. Are you resisting God?" he whispered.

"No," I said. I saw sympathy in his eyes. Nevertheless, he moved on. A knot developed in my stomach. Was God rejecting me?

Ed prayed with some others and then came back to me. Before he said anything, I started to cry. He said, "Yes, go there. I think God wants to reveal something to you."

I didn't see or hear anything from God. All I knew was that tears flooded out because of anguish deep in my heart. I went to sit on a chair by myself.

After the church members left, Ed and I asked God for answers. Within a few minutes, Ed said, "I hear, *Right up to it. Stand right up to it.* In my spirit I see a steel fire door, like those used in warehouses to prevent fires from spreading. Those doors have a heat sensor; if the sensor gets too hot, a switch flips, the door shuts, and that part of the building is protected. Similarly, there's a door on your heart, and it has an automatic safety mechanism. Under certain conditions, when a violation or a trigger of some kind occurs, the door reflexively shuts and closes off your heart. This door on your heart is real, but it's not your door. It belongs to the devil. He installed it to operate as a weapon against you. This door acts as if it's a safety device, but it's not; it prevents you from fully opening your heart to Jesus."

I asked Ed how to get rid of it. He didn't know as God became silent about the door. We switched gears and prayed about the anguish I experienced earlier. Ed recalled that Jesus felt anguish in the garden of Gethsemane. The word *Gethsemane* means the oil press. Jesus went there to force, or press His flesh to submit to His spirit. Twice He fervently prayed, but He didn't accomplish His goal. He told Peter, "The spirit indeed is willing, but the flesh is weak" (Matt. 26:41). Jesus prayed a third time—until His flesh submitted to God's will (Matt. 26:44).

"I guess God's will is not always easy or joyous," I commented.

"That's right. In Matthew 6:38, Jesus said, 'My soul is exceedingly sorrowful, even to death.'"

As we talked about Jesus's anguish, my spirit felt upset. We didn't know if God had led me to my own Gethsemane, but we knew He was leading me, one step at a time, to a higher place. To climb the next step, it was necessary to get rid of more of myself. Yes, I was in the oil press. I would be there for a while.

Echoes of rejection haunted me. I tried to handle the anxiety that started to consume me since God passed by me, but it continued to build. I needed to hear God say He still loved me and to reassure me that I was still accepted. I asked Ed to pray with me.

As revelation came, Ed said, "When you were a little girl, Satan trained you to react with fear and anxiety, shame and guilt, and to blame yourself for everything. Since you've been conditioned, you automatically respond in this manner. This puts you in subjection to him and he's been like a puppet master ever since. To succeed in your garden experience, for the old man to die, you first have to accept that the devil has preconditioned you to react with fear and self-debasement."

I told Ed I was starting to grasp this, but it seemed impossible to completely understand how thoroughly the devil had trained me. I was not to worry. In my own Gethsemane, God would show me what the devil had planted. The preconditioned responses would get exposed and uprooted. They would wither and die.

Ed said, "Even today, God is revealing an area you have been conditioned in: performance-based love. Satan told lies and used people's actions to teach you that if you performed well enough, then, and only then, would you be loved. Eventually your performance-based picture of love morphed into a performance-based picture of salvation."

Satan told lies and used people's actions to teach you that if you performed well enough, then, and only then, would you be loved.

Ed was right. Performing for love was a normal part of my life. And I automatically applied it to my relationship with God. I unconsciously thought that if I performed well; went to church, prayed enough, and said and did the right things, then God would love me. I guess I was trying to prevent God from rejecting me.

Ed explained that no one can work to prevent that. It is part of the devil's deception, to have us spend time and energy trying to accomplish the impossible—performing to obtain God's acceptance.

"When God was silent last week, I thought He had rejected me," I said.

Ed pointed out that Satan helped me along by whispering that God had turned His back on me. "As you gave Satan your ear, he pulled out your old sad songs of rejection and played them until you found yourself engaged in an intimate slow dance with him. By taking your eyes off God and His promises, you could no longer see His truths."

Ed encouraged, "Don't be too hard on yourself. Even though God touched on this topic months ago, it is okay to need a reminder about what God's love is based on. God won't change His mind about you, and you can't make Him. His love is not determined by what you do, or don't do—you can't earn it. It's unconditional! You've applied situational ethics to your relationship with God; *if* I do this, *then* God will love me. But Romans 5:8 says that God loved you and sent Jesus to die for you when you were a sinner. He would certainly still love you if you had resisted Him.

It is okay to need a reminder about what God's love is based on.

"You also need to realize God's love for you is not based on His performance. His apparent lack of performance last week is what got you started down this road of rejection. Furthermore, by believing God had forsaken you, you didn't believe His Word, and you didn't believe in His unconditional love—ironically you rejected part of God."

My heart felt remorseful and I didn't know what to say.

God prompted Ed to say more. "As a child, fear of rejection was embedded into your heart, and wounds from past rejections have not healed. Though these wounds are old, they're still active and festering like newly infected cuts. The devil just has to lightly touch these unhealed wounds and you flinch in pain, automatically believing God has rejected you.

"These wounds cause an automatic knee-jerk reaction to perceived rejection. Your fear that God turned His back on you was triggered by the pain of past rejection that you carry in your heart. To disable the knee-jerk response, the pain has to go."

"How do I get rid of it?" I asked.

Ed responded that I had to look into my heart, see that the old beliefs of performance-based love and acceptance were still there, and then decide to refuse them. He said it would be like literally reaching in, pulling out the lies, and throwing them in the trash! Then the wounds could heal.

Your pain may be hidden from you, but it's not hidden from God—He intimately understands the depth of your wounds.

"I don't want to touch these lies or even look at them," I replied.

Ed said, "I sense intense passion. It's the passion God has for your heart and for your wounds. Your pain may be hidden from you, but it's not hidden from God—He intimately understands the depth of your wounds. Your pain is alive to Him. Your pain is in Him. The longer you have it, the more He hurts. His love is so intense and fervent that when you're in pain, He's in pain."

I prayed about my wounds, but couldn't uncover the pain because the anxiety continued to rise. I called Ed and cried about my life. Afterward, I felt guilty for being weak, but God was merciful and brought 2 Corinthians 12:9 to my mind. "My grace is sufficient for you, for My strength is made perfect in weakness." God didn't mind my weakness, but I was sorry about and ashamed of my behavior.

After we talked on the phone, Ed came over to pray. He said, "The word *shame* has been echoing in my spirit. Did you know that your life has been built around and based on shame? It's what your parents taught you to believe about yourself."

"And my shame-based life at home was reinforced by my childhood church, other people, and the sinful things I had done," I added.

Ed told me it was time to dispute my shame-based image. "The first step is to admit to yourself and confess to God that you were wrong to live under a canopy of shame. Since Jesus took your sins and guilt at the time of your salvation, you can't keep the shame. It's not compatible! Your self-portrait is still based on your past experiences, especially what your parents said and did. That old ugly picture of you still hangs on the wall of your heart. It has to be taken down and thrown away."

I said, "I'm willing to get rid of that picture of shame, but I don't know how."

Ed said, "I have a vision of a grassy field. A path has been worn through it by the animals that walk there. A trap with food has been laid on the path. When an animal walks by, it takes the bait. *Caught.* Now the trap setter can do what he wants with the captured prey."

Ed looked at me, "The enemy has laid a camouflaged trap in your path. The path is your everyday life, the place you inhabit. God is exposing the trap.

"The snare is the shame in your heart and when triggered, it takes you captive. You're spring-loaded to shame because your life experiences have painted that color on your heart."

"How can I paint myself a different color?" I asked.

"First, the old paint has to be scraped off, which means giving up your former identity. Let's start by examining *shame.* It usually happens because of the presence of others. If I were alone in the woods and stepped in dog poop, I would just scrape it off my shoe. I might be irritated, but I wouldn't be ashamed because no one saw it. If that happened on the way into church, my reaction would likely be different because of my concern about what others might think."

Ed continued, "Now we need to study the word *base*. A base holds something up. A lamp can't stand upright without a solid base. If the base is uneven, the lamp will fall over at the slightest touch because its foundation is unstable."

Ed stopped walking and stood next to me. He gently said, "Your base is to be righteousness because Jesus redeemed you from guilt and shame. Your seven years with God; the prayers, tears, joy, speaking in tongues, and revelations haven't changed your base of shame. As you've grown in Christ, you've grown crooked—because your base is tilted."

"Help me to eliminate the tilted base of shame, the spring-loaded trap in my path," I pleaded.

"How does shame come?" Ed asked.

After thinking for a moment, I said, "My mom used to say, 'Shame on you' when I did or said something she didn't approve of."

"She put a curse on you when she spoke those words!" Ed exclaimed. He immediately prayed, "Right now I break those curses that Denise's mother spoke over her. They are broken; they have no value, no power.

"Now I want to anoint your ears with oil." As he did that, he said, "I anoint your ears to hear the truth and to take away the foundation of shame in your thoughts."

As Ed walked around me, he said, "No more shame. It's a lie. You cannot believe the lie, you must reject the lies you heard. No shame on you, no shame in you, and no condemnation. You will hear the righteousness of God, and you will hear the truth of God. You will not be shame-based anymore. Your mother's words are broken because the Word of God is sharper than any two-edged sword; revealing the truth and cutting out the shame. There is no shame on you Denise. There is glory on you, grace on you, peace on you. The peace of God is in you, the glory of God is in you, and God's glory is coming out of you. Righteousness is in you, and righteousness is upon you. You have peace and glory, and no shame. Your foundation is straight with God."

As Ed spoke those words of God's glory, grace, peace, and righteousness on me, God's power hit me like gusts of wind from Heaven. As each word swept against me, I was blown backward a step. God filled me with His blessings, and as they entered my heart, the picture of shame that hung there was torn away. My base was no longer tilted.

God continued to impart knowledge to Ed. "Though your heart is now free from the curse of shame and also filled with God's goodness, you need to fully understand that you're not shame-based any longer and that your base is righteousness. You need to believe that because of Jesus, you can stand naked in front of God, smile at Him, and have no shame. You've been washed in the blood of Christ and are clothed in a robe of righteousness. Whether you believe it yet or not, you have no shame—Jesus has taken it away, as far as the east is from the west" (Ps. 103:12).

After quietly conversing with God, Ed added, "To change your beliefs, you have to focus on the pre-conditioning; your mother's lies."

My mom was an illegitimate child. She must have grown up shame-based herself. Sadly, she raised me to be like her, painting me with the same color of shame.

Ed said, "This lie has been a powerful force. After your mom filled you with shame, Satan used that shame to try to kill you."

Ed was right. As a teenager and young adult, I was filled with shame, so much so that I wanted to die. That's why I used drugs, drank alcohol excessively, and put myself in dangerous situations. My behavior brought more shame, and it reinforced that I was guilty and unworthy of love. I hated myself. I even carved the word *hate* on my leg with a knife.

When God's light shines on darkness, the enemy's lies become worthless. God exposed this lie of shame because He wanted it out of my heart. The trap, the curse of shame was broken, but I was not yet completely free.

God's attention suppressed my anxiety, and my heart felt lighter since that curse was gone. A week later, when Ed and I got together to pray, I was feeling great about things and requested that we pray specifically that I would have more intimacy with God.

> Greater intimacy with God will only come if you trust Him more.

As we began, Ed said, "Greater intimacy with God will only come if you trust Him more. In my spirit I see a trapeze artist. You are to become like one who walks the tight ropes; fully entrusting God with your life. He is the wire whose strength holds you."

"I know God holds me up. He caused me to run back to Him, He rescued me from the enemy, and He's sustaining me through my trials. God has been faithful. He's never failed to give me the answers and the peace I need. I've trusted God through hard times, and I'm learning to trust Him even more."

Ed challenged, "Why do you openly speak God's praises, yet not acknowledge your commendable qualities? You have diligently sought after God, your faith has grown, and your understanding of Him has increased, but you ignore the good things you've done. Your self-portrait is still skewed. You have a Picasso-style picture of yourself and it needs to change to the image God has of you. You need to see yourself as a beautiful princess of the King."

"Sometimes I do," I said.

"Sometimes isn't enough. As you strive to see yourself in this new picture, you only walk out so far on the high wire before you turn back and default to the Picasso painting. This is part of killing the old man; doing away with who you think you are. You need to take that Picasso person and nail him, or in your case her, to the cross. She's not the real you. She's an imposter.

"God wants you to conform back to the person He created you to be. That means God has to take you out of Satan's mold, grind you into powder, mix you with the Holy Spirit, and pour you back into your original container—the image and likeness of Him."

I knew I was made in the image of God, yet to my heart it seemed impossible to change my self-image. I had believed the lies for forty years, some of them buried pretty deep, and I had no tools to remove them.

Ed agreed with me that I couldn't do it—*God* was repainting my picture.

After praying a while, I paused and told Ed, "The last few weeks, the thought, *I have trouble going to God,* has been resonating in my mind. I don't know if this is my thought or the enemy talking."

Ed proclaimed, "God says it's you. You know you can't approach Him with your Picasso image and you don't want Him to look at you because you think you're ugly inside."

"I'm confused," I said. "There seems to be two of me."

"Yes. There's the new you who races toward the throne room and wants more of God, and there's the old shameful you who hides from God's presence. In my spirit I see the image of a hand holding a picture. When the new you approaches God, the devil brings out the Picasso picture and holds it in front of you. Your natural eyes can't see the image, but your heart can, and you back away from God. Do you know that you're beautiful to God?"

"My heart really struggles to believe that," I admitted.

Ed instructed me to say over and over, "I am beautiful to God on the inside and the outside." I recoiled at the thought of saying this, but I said it again and again until I could finally say it without resistance, until I accepted it as truth. I turned to Ed and said, "I believe that I'm beautiful to God, but I'm still not beautiful to myself."

"That's because Satan, your supreme criticizer, taught you to be critical of yourself. Over the years, he's reminded you of what you've done wrong, told you how bad, ugly, and worthless you are, and that you deserve to be mistreated. You heard it so often that you believe it, and have even said those things about yourself. Fortunately, there is freedom in the truth, and that's where God is leading you."

Ed continued, "You've accepted that you're beautiful to God, so you can stand before Him naked and unashamed with a smile on your face and in your heart. You can have an intimate heart-to-heart, shameless-to-shameless, trust-to-trust, love-to-love relationship with Him. God is your Father, you came from Him, and you're part of Him."

God is beautiful. Since I am a part of God, I am beautiful too!

I'm part of God?! God is beautiful. Since I am a part of God, I am beautiful too! What an important truth.

Ed said, "Oh no. God has a warning for you. Your mom instilled shame into you all those years ago. Now Satan will use your mom to try to shame your daughter. You cannot let her shame Hannah."

Dread grabbed my heart. I had never thought of this! I would have to lay some strict boundaries for my mom. It was crucial that she _never_ speak those demonic words to my daughter.

I felt a little intimidated at the thought of confronting my mom, but if could stand naked in front of God, I could certainly stand up to my mom. And within a week, I did. As Hannah played on the playground, I talked with my mom. I told her how her words had covered me in shame. She was surprised, and though she didn't completely understand, she was sorry for hurting me. She promised never to speak shame to Hannah or me again.

Fear Not

For God has not given us a spirit of fear,
but of power and of love and of a sound mind.
—2 Timothy 1:7

SEVEN MONTHS HAD PASSED since the night of the crisis. Although I had made so much progress, I was getting discouraged because I was still hearing negative thoughts about God and Jesus. I wanted to know why this was still happening. Ed and I came to God in prayer to seek answers.

Within minutes, revelation knowledge came through Ed. "You've been accepting bribes. These enticements are whispered suggestions from the devil and they're so soft you don't initially detect them. You unwittingly follow the first one, then the next one, and the next. Each one is designed to move you just a little bit farther from God's light. As the devil slowly edges you into the shadows, you don't perceive how dark it has become, until you hear the destructive comments and feel the adverse effects.

"When you finally notice the negative words, you don't fight against them, because relative to other attacks you've experienced, this is mild. By letting the devil continue to speak to you, you've compromised. You think since it's not a big assault, it's all right, but little by little it continues until you become surrounded by darkness and can't find your way back to the light. It's important that you recognize the whispered suggestions for what they are and then do something about them."

> *By letting the devil continue to speak to you, you've compromised.*

I replied, "At times, the devil's lying voice is a constant noise in my ear. Other times, I know he's speaking, but his words aren't clear enough for me to decipher. What is the reason for this difference?"

"Ah, I see that Lord," Ed said and then turned to face me. "You're ready and willing to fight the devil—most of the time. When you're not willing, the enemy's voice comes through loud and clear."

My Friday night routine came to mind. That was the night I devoted quality time to Hannah. On those special nights, I put my shield and sword down so I could play with my daughter. In doing so, I established boundaries for when I would fight and when I would disengage. Unfortunately, the devil had no boundaries, and he was exploiting the fact that I did. He knew I wouldn't give up time with my daughter to fight him in prayer. He knew I laid my weapons down—a perfect time to attack.

I also told Ed that I didn't fight at my job. I couldn't battle the devil at work because people were around and I couldn't pray like I did at home.

Ed responded, "You can withstand the enemy at work. You can quietly pray when you're alone, think on God's Word and speak it when you have the chance, and you can close your mind to the devil.

I'm sure you block some of the enemy's thoughts, but it's imperative that you disarm the thoughts that get in."

Ed looked up a verse and read it out loud. "Second Corinthians 10:5 says, 'Casting down arguments and every high thing that exalts itself against the knowledge of God, bringing every thought into captivity to the obedience of Christ.' When you hear the devil's voice, even the soft suggestions, you have to take his words captive. This means

Since you have authority over every thought, you can either accept or reject each one.

you can't believe what he says or go down the path he tries to lead you on. Since you have authority over every thought, you can either accept or reject each one."

I said, "One of the distressing thoughts I've been hearing for months is *I reject Jesus*."

"That's not your thought. Satan wants you to think it is, so he uses the weapon of first person language. Let's defuse those fear-filled words right now! What would happen if you actually did reject Jesus?"

"I'd go to Hell?" I guessed.

"No. You could repent, and God would restore you. And to really reject Jesus, you would have to verbally confess your rejection of Him. For that to come out of your mouth, it would have to be in your heart, as Luke 6:45 says, 'For out of the abundance of the heart his mouth speaks.'"

That was comforting to me because I knew that was not in my heart. I knew I would never tell Jesus to leave.

Once again, the truth had set me free. The *I reject Jesus* had lost its power. Some time passed with no new problems, so Ed and I prayed just to hear what God might have to say. Prompted by the Holy Spirit, Ed asked me, "Have you given God permission to forgive you?"

"What are you talking about?" I asked.

God's wisdom flowed through Ed. "As a child, you couldn't be around your dad without fear of incrimination, and you were usually rejected and condemned by him. That became your picture of a father. Now with your heavenly Father, you unconsciously wait for Him to find you guilty or to reject you. The endless wondering if today is the day God will drop the hammer on you needs to stop. That corrupt building block is part of the foundation of your life, but it's unsound and needs to go."

Getting rid of this awful feeling appealed to me, but I didn't know how to do that.

Ed continued, "To remove it, to eliminate the fear of your heavenly Father, you need to trust that God won't forsake you—but there's a problem. The pure water of God's Word is muddied by the pollution of your past."

Interactions with my dad had been unpredictable. Sometimes he would be calm, but many times he would erupt in anger or disapproval. I was always nervous in his presence, never knowing how he would react.

Ed said, "Even though your dad's behavior was unreliable, you trusted his statements were true. When your dad or mom said 'You should be ashamed of yourself' or 'You are stupid,' you believed them. Their parenting not only skewed your view of self, but how you regard God as well.

"God is your Abba Father (Rom. 8:15). He's like a parent, so you've unintentionally applied your parents' conduct to Him, but those norms can't apply—God has perfect parenting skills. You've dishonored God by viewing Him through the lens of your parents, expecting Him to behave like them. On an unconscious level, their detrimental parenting has made you fearful of approaching your heavenly Father, and is preventing you from trusting His character. You need to trust that God is gracious and merciful to forgive you and lovingly holds you in the palm of His hand. God doesn't need your permission to forgive you; He has already forgiven you. God merely wants you to see that you aren't trusting of His forgiveness."

You've dishonored God by viewing Him through the lens of your parents, expecting Him to behave like them.

One day as Ed and I visited about how things were going, he referred to my dad as my father.

"Don't ever call my dad my father again," I said firmly.

Ed was taken aback, but then having received a revelation from God, said that the reason it was offensive for me to think of my dad as my father was because I now saw God as my Father.

Ed was right. And I didn't want them called by the same name because they were so different. I didn't want to associate them with each other.

Ed said, "I sense there's something about your dad still hidden in your heart. We should pray about it." A few minutes into our session, the Holy Spirit spoke through Ed. "Your dad didn't show you how a good father treats his children."

That simple statement hit me hard. I fell to my knees and started to weep. Through my tears I cried out, "He hated me, he hated me." The hatred I'd had for my dad was gone, but now God revealed that my dad had hated me. It wasn't just that he didn't want kids; he actually hated me. He despised me just because I was alive. I told Ed, "I feel strange inside. I don't know whether to laugh or keep crying, if I feel more alive or dead."

Ed replied, "I think something in you died."

God had exposed another painful truth, and He put another dent in the chain. As He worked on freeing the wounded girl in my heart, our relationship was becoming more intimate. Intimacy is what I had always wanted from my earthly father, but never experienced. I knew my heavenly Father didn't hate me, but I didn't yet know how well He wanted to treat me.

I felt quite good for several weeks. Then some feelings of depression started. After being unsuccessful in fighting off this unexplained sorrow, I asked Ed to pray with me.

As we entered our prayer room, I recounted a devotional I had read recently. "Every good and every perfect gift is from above and comes down from the Father of lights" (James 1:17). I told Ed it helped me see Jesus in a new way. "He's my perfect gift from God. I have such a hard time accepting gifts."

Ed said, "God brought that verse to your memory so He could help you. You're averse to receiving gifts because you think you're not worthy of them. To get a gift you would have to be special or good and you don't see yourself that way."

"When I get a gift, I feel indebted to the one who gives it because gifts often come with conditions or obligations attached to them," I added.

Ed replied, "God's gift of Jesus is not like any other gift you've received. Jesus is an undeserved gift and given without conditions. And God is not like other gift givers. His motives are pure, not selfish. The term *gift* was a trigger that set off a hidden landmine in your heart. Now that trigger is disabled."

"My heart feels light again. I've unreservedly accepted Jesus as my perfect gift from God!" I declared.

Ed smiled and said, "I'm not surprised. You always take hold of what God reveals to you."

Before Ed left, I wanted to tell him something else. I said, "I've noticed that sometimes my gait changes as I walk and pray. I take a step forward with my right foot and then bring my left foot alongside it, like a bride walks down the aisle."

Ed said, "That's a physical manifestation of the work God is doing in you. You're the bride of Christ! You are a bride walking toward her Bridegroom!"

We prayed in tongues until Ed stopped and turned to me. "I heard you say, *Where are you?*" Operating in a word of knowledge, Ed replaced that with, "Where are the nine?"

"Ouch!" I cried. "I felt a stab in my heart when you said that."

"I'm referring to the ten lepers Jesus healed. After being healed, nine of them didn't go back to thank or glorify God (Luke 17:12-18). *Where are you?* is a question from God to you. It's not an accusation; God wants you to see where you are."

I didn't know where I was. Perhaps God would tell us more later, in His timing.

Ed and I were talking on the phone when I made some comments that implied I thought sex was distasteful. Ed remarked, "The devil has twisted what God created to be good and made it offensive in your heart."

I told him I didn't care because I had no intention of getting married. Two nights later, I dreamed that a godly man I admired tried to have sex with me. I was repulsed.

The next time Ed came over to pray, I told him about my dream and then said, "I have regrets from my past, but I'm not going to talk to you about them."

"You know God was there watching," he replied.

I winced before groaning, "Don't say that." Ed saw the guilt and shame on my face. "I thought that was gone," I grumbled.

Ed explained, "Shame surfaced because you still feel guilty about some lewd things you've done. But the person you are now—a purified virgin cleansed from all unrighteousness by the blood of Christ—is different from who you were then. The person you were in the past ceases to exist. She's dead because you've been born again. You're a new person. It's not just a Bible cliché, but a spiritual reality. And the new you is just as righteous as Jesus."

I didn't know what to say, so I began walking around and praying in tongues. Ed stood off to the side and remained deep in thought. After a minute or so, he said, "You keep saying, 'Must clean it out.' God told me that you've accepted His forgiveness of your sins, however you haven't forgiven yourself. The dream you had was a manifestation of the enemy's lie. The lie isn't about sex, but about the guilt and shame you still believe is yours. You agree with the lie because you still see yourself as the old you, the one who carries her evidence of guilt and shame. To release the shackles of self-condemnation, you need to distinguish yourself from the old you and from her guilt."

"How do I do that?" I asked.

"Acts 11:9 says, 'What God has cleansed you must not call common.' Since Jesus has washed you with His blood and gave you right standing with God, you can't see yourself as unclean. You have to see yourself as sinless. To accomplish that, you need to replace the guilt and shame that lives in your heart with the truth of God's Word. It's essential that you find out what the Bible says, believe it, and then speak and meditate on God's truths. This will discredit the lies and bring you to a place of decision. Will you believe what God says, or believe the lies that hold you hostage to guilt and shame?"

"This captive wants freedom!" I declared.

As we finished praying, I joked, "Don't come too close to me, I haven't taken a shower yet today."

"*Sweet smelling*. You smell sweet to God. Do you remember when you first held Hannah? You said she had an unpleasant odor to her because the caretakers at the orphanage had only cleansed her with a cloth. That's a picture of you. You had a stench when you came to God, but you have been bathed in the blood of Jesus and now you smell sweet and fresh—just as your daughter did after her first real bath."

I was a sweet aroma to God! What a beautiful reality.

I was amazed at what God was doing in my life! Each time Ed and I prayed, God revealed secrets and destroyed lies. At times they were more dramatic than others, but individually and collectively they all impacted my heart.

The devil's attacks had gradually diminished and I thought this battle was almost over. Now war was waged on my sleep. This was different from the insomnia I'd had when I was anxious about my salvation. At that time my mind was filled with fear and torment. Now my mind was peaceful, but my body couldn't relax. As I lay in bed, my body felt like it had enough energy to run a marathon. At times my heart beat so fast, and my extremities tingled. I waited two to three hours for my body to calm down enough for sleep to come, then after an hour or two of sleep, I'd wake up alert, and the pattern would repeat. After a few nights in a row of this, I asked Ed to pray with me about it.

I told Ed, "All I want is a quick fix. I need God to tell us what the problem is so we can correct it, and I can move on with my life."

Ed said I wasn't going to get that today, that God expected me to engage. "He wants you to take up the position He's called you to. Part of that position requires you to carry yourself and not be supported by me all the time. You've been depending on me too much."

I looked at the floor, "That wasn't my intent."

Ed reassured me, "Needing support has been your default position. But now God requires you to go beyond your self-imposed limits and be stronger then you've ever been. Joel 3:10 says, 'Let the weak say, I am strong.' You are armed with the Holy Spirit, the sword of the Spirit, and the shield of faith. You have to hold your ground against Satan by not retreating."

"That's not what I hoped to hear. Still, I'll put my armor on."

I told Ed someone was contending for my sleep, but I didn't know if it was the devil attacking me or if God had started a work in me. I needed discernment. Then I would know whose signature was attached to the event, and I would know whether to fight or yield.

I told Ed what I knew. The "what if" questions were back; what if I can't function, what if I lose my job, and what if I can't take care of my daughter. These questions were familiar flaming arrows of the devil, but they came as a consequence of no sleep, they weren't the cause.

Ed said, "You automatically try to understand problems with your mind and reasoning. Listen to 1 Corinthians 2:14. It tells us, 'But the natural man does not receive the things of the Spirit of God, for they are foolishness to him; nor can he know them, because they are spiritually discerned.' To understand this problem, you need to spiritually discern it, rather than use your mind to look for clues and rationalize logical evidence. Your default to the natural man for answers needs to change. That too is part of your old man dying."

I'd experienced some degree of spiritual discernment. Once I sensed evil in a man when I stood next to him. Another time, the evil presence in a book was so strong that I reflexively threw it down. I didn't ask for those moments of discernment. They just came to me. I asked Ed, "Why do I have it at times and not at other times?"

Ed replied, "You don't always walk in the spirit. You yield to your spirit at times, but you're not supposed to just yield. Galatians 5:25 says, 'If we live in the Spirit, let us also walk in the Spirit.' God gave you your spirit and your mind, and He expects you to use both. But He wants your born-again spirit to dominate because your mind is too easily influenced by the devil and the world's ways."

We didn't get further insight about my sleep issue, but I had God's promise of Proverb 3:24. "When you lie down, you will not be afraid; yes, you will lie down and your sleep will be sweet."

With two weeks of almost no sleep, I thought my life was about to spin out of control again. What would happen to Hannah if I couldn't take care of her? My relationship with my sister was almost non-existent now, so I couldn't rely on her as a safety net like I did before. My anxiety level escalated again, so I did the only thing I knew to do; I asked Ed to pray with me.

After I explained my fear to Ed, he asked me to face my worst and somewhat irrational fear: what if I could no longer care for Hannah and she had to be returned to an orphanage in China? I felt panic-stricken. "She'd be alone and scared. I don't want her to be like I used to be!" I cried.

Ed put his hand on my shoulder and said, "The pain of being like an orphan in your own home is a festering sore in your heart. This wound was invisible to you, but Satan is keenly aware of it and he's taking the trauma of your childhood experience and twisting it into 'What if this happens to my daughter?'

"Let's look at what could potentially happen. With ongoing lack of sleep, maybe you wouldn't be able to care for Hannah adequately, and she would have to live with a friend or relative."

I chimed in and said that I could get fired for not doing my job well. Then I wouldn't have the finances needed to care for her. The devil's "what if" question was valid, but he was bombarding me with it to maximize my stress level. Satan was pushing me toward failure and the sure inability to function.

Ed stared at the carpet and said, "In my spirit I see God holding your heart in the palm of His hand. He's moved His thumb away to show you this pain; it's time for healing. You need to apply the salve of forgiveness. It's vital that you forgive your mom and dad for putting pain into you—otherwise the wound can't heal and the fear of Hannah's life becoming like yours will continue to have power."

Ed asked me, "Can this ever happen to you again?"

"No." I said emphatically.

Ed concurred. "Consciously realizing the wound can't be re-peated will make it easier to let go of the pain and fear. You're no longer a vulnerable little girl they can hurt."

Ed led me in a prayer of forgiveness: "I forgive you, Mom and Dad, for causing this deep-rooted pain, pain that you didn't need to give me, pain that became part of my life. I forgive both of you for harming me and for the wrongs you've committed against me. I forgive you for the tears you caused me to shed. I reject the pain you caused; I cast it out. I set down that pain and walk away from it because it's no longer mine. I don't want it and it can't come back. I put the pain in the grave with the girl I used to be."

My forgiveness of them freed me from the pain of what they had done

My parents hadn't made restitution with me. They weren't even aware of the harm they had caused. But my forgiveness of them freed me from the pain of what they had done and allowed the wound to heal.

After Ed and I finished praying, God impressed upon me that as He was healing my wounds, He was also building a fortress around my heart. Now, not all of Satan's arrows would penetrate; some of them would ricochet off the fortress.

A month had passed since my sleep problems began. Surely this could not be a work of God. A few nights here and there I got decent sleep, but most nights were sheer torture. In addition to my body running for the finish line, my mind had entered the race as well. I spent eight hours a night in bed and slept about three. One night, the devil pulled out a new trick to steal my sleep; I was awakened by the smell of burning flesh. I was repulsed, though not afraid—I knew this signature.

I called Ed and asked him to come over to pray. As we circled around the room, I said, "I'm battle weary due to lack of sleep. How much longer is this going to last?"

"I don't know, but I know the enemy can't defeat you, and this battle belongs to God (1 Sam. 17:47). I also know that God can't give you the victory unless you enter into the battle." He went on to encourage me, "You've had many victories already and your victories are everlasting—you never go back to the same battle. Sometimes you've battled in the same area, but fought it from a different angle."

"I know my triumphs have come only through the hand of God. I'm relying on Him to help me win this fight as well."

After a few minutes of praying, Ed asked, "What would happen to you if you died today?"

I was surprised by his question, but I answered, "I would stand before Jesus and I think He would accept me. I admit that I would be nervous standing before Jesus. I would likely hang my head and hope for a positive response. I guess I'm still a little afraid He might reject me on that day."

Ed said, "God held you in His hand when you were like a newborn kitten; weak and fragile. Now the helpless kitten He lifted up, protected, loved, and cared for, is growing up. The only difference between you then and now is that you're more obedient and trusting—so God's heart toward you has not changed."

I told Ed that on a good day, I know I belong to God and I'm confident of where I'll go when I die. On a bad day, when I'm tired or discouraged, or my words or actions aren't as pleasant as I would like, I don't have that assurance. When I don't perform well, I have to remind myself of God's truths because I begin to worry about my relationship with God.

Ed replied, "You become insecure when life doesn't go well because the devil has trained you to have an automatic reflex—to see yourself in a negative light. You'll have to retrain the conditioned response, as life's trials will never completely stop."

Ed looked up a verse and read, "Isaiah 26:3 says, 'You will keep him in perfect peace, whose mind is stayed on You, because he trusts in You.' Your job is to keep your mind on Christ. It's not your job to try to have peace. You'll have God's perfect peace if you keep your mind on Him, trust Him, and believe His Word rather than those old reflexive responses."

Your job is to keep your mind on Christ. It's not your job to try to have peace.

"This word from God confirms my new endeavor," I replied excitedly. "To help me fall asleep lately, I've started dwelling on God's Word rather than let my mind run in any direction it chooses. I'm meditating on a shortened version of Psalm 4:8. In my head I slowly repeat, 'I lie down in peace and sleep' over and over. Initially this was difficult, but with practice and much redirection, it now prevents other thoughts from entering my mind, and it brings peace to my body, which allows sleep to come. I have to do this every time I wake up, which is many times a night."

Ed and I prayed in tongues until Ed declared, "You just said, 'You must be obeyed today.' Oh, I see that Lord," Ed muttered.

Ed went on to explain that when I was a child, my dad's commands usually brought fear or pain. That caused my view of authority and commands to be skewed. God didn't want my picture of authority to look like screaming sirens and flashing red lights. He wanted me to realize that I could be commanded to lie down in green pastures beside still waters, as Psalm 23 says. God wanted me to trust that His authority was good, unlike the authority my dad exercised over me. And because I saw authority as abusive, I was reluctant to be authoritative myself.

I agreed. When I exercised my authority, I got a bad taste in my mouth. I was not really against authority though, but against abuse of authority, which I mistakenly saw as true authority. As I went through this relearning process, I realized God's authority was safe and wrapped in love. I decided to be like my heavenly Father. I would exercise my authority, yet not be abusive.

When Ed and I prayed the next time, God continued His lesson on authority. Ed began, "You've been commanding demons to leave you alone, but God says you're still not doing it properly or with full authority. When someone is in authority, they don't say 'I command you'; they just give the command. When you use those words, you tip off the devil that you're trying to step into something you're not sure you have.

"You can't step into authority or take authority over evil spirits because you already have it, and it came from Jesus. As a joint heir with Christ, you have His authority, and you don't need to tell the enemy that. Satan knows he can't change the Word of God, the work of the Cross, or the power of the Holy Spirit. He is well aware that he has to submit to those who are Christ's when they properly exercise God's authority."

I agreed that I could change what I said, but wondered why I was not walking in God's full authority.

Ed explained, "There are two reasons. One is your childhood, and the other is your past training in the church. Both those environments taught you that you didn't have authority, and you should submit. When you gave your life to Jesus, He took you out of Satan's kingdom and brought you into His (Col. 1:13). Now that you live in Jesus's kingdom, you walk in His authority. You have the ability to command demons to flee, and you have authority over all the works of the enemy. Luke 10:19 says, 'Behold, I give you the authority to trample on serpents and scorpions, and over all the power of the enemy, and nothing shall by any means hurt you.'"

Ed asked me if I knew what an ambassador does. When I admitted that I didn't, he asked me to look up 2 Corinthians 5:20 and read it out loud. "Sure," I said. "Now then, we are ambassadors for Christ, as though God were pleading through us: we implore you on Christ's behalf, be reconciled to God."

Ed explained that when a country's president selects an ambassador, he chooses someone he trusts to speak for him and who will do what he's been appointed to do. Before the ambassador leaves, the president gives him instructions about what he is to accomplish while in that country. When the ambassador goes, he carries the authority of the office of the president and he does and says what the president—who is his final authority—has commissioned him to do and say.

Ed went on, "Likewise, as an ambassador for Christ, you're commissioned by the King. You have no authority of your own, the King gives you authority to speak His Word, and His Word carries the authority. As an ambassador for Christ, demons, who are ambassadors for Satan, have to obey you—because your King defeated their king."

As I pondered this, Ed announced, "In my spirit I see an image of a woman yelling at you. She scolded you in order to beat you into a place of submission. But she wasn't the one who positioned you; Satan worked through her voice, her anger, and her authority. She had been assigned by him to turn your future in the wrong direction—to keep you from going where God wants you to go. Because of her display of power, you cowered in the corner and accepted the direction in which she pointed you. That took you off the path of God and into a garbage heap. That's not where God wants you!

"You're supposed to be on the path that God exquisitely designed just for you. He paved it Himself. Only you can walk this path; it was built for you long before you were born and your name is on it. The name on your path isn't Denise. On it is your name that's written in Heaven, the name on the white stone you'll receive some day, the name only God knows" (Revelation 2:17).

Ed continued, "God is giving me a vision of your path. I see steppingstones. They're fourteen inch brown square tiles with beveled edges, set on flat ground in a perfectly straight line. The stones don't touch each other; the space between them is as far apart as your natural steps. As a matter of fact, the distance between the stones changes as you grow spiritually. The stones are places of support, and the light of Jesus shines on the path to guide you. As your feet land on the stones, you walk toward the white stone with your name on it. God expects you to walk at your natural pace on the path that holds your destiny. You're not required to run the path, and no extraordinary effort is needed to walk it—only submission to God."

Ed wiped his eyes with his sleeve, and his voice became hoarse as he continued. "Though you've spent much of your life off the path, God didn't allow one blade of grass to grow over your stepping stones. The dark green grass with wide flat tops hadn't just been cut—it had been manicured. Angels trimmed it as they expectantly waited for you. Once you started walking your path, the angels were commanded to keep it clear of hazards and obstacles. They also provide protection on each side. Each step you take brings you nearer to God and closer to attaining 'Well done, good and faithful servant'

(Matthew 25:21). The love God has put into creating your path is overwhelming; it's excruciatingly intimate, beautiful, and peaceful."

As I looked at Ed's awestruck countenance, I could only imagine the beauty he beheld. I silently wondered why God hadn't shown my path to me.

Ed said, "You've accepted your role as an ambassador for Christ and you've already been walking the path laid before you. As you forge ahead, you carry something powerful in your heart. Though you walk your path as an ambassador, part of you won't stand tall. This part of you is the young girl who learned to survive threatening circumstances by cowering in a corner. You created some bad habits in that corner, but that's where you coped with danger and you learned that position to protect yourself. Although it enabled you to remain alive in your previous environment, you can't walk your stepping stones if you're trembling in the corner.

"That part of you should never have existed. She was fabricated and preconditioned by Satan to get you to step off your path and prevent you from walking out God's plan for your life. She was deceived into living in the garbage heap in the corner—where she can't do what an ambassador is supposed to do. Unfortunately she's been a reality for so long, you still identify yourself with her."

I told Ed I wanted to get rid of the girl who crouches in fear in the corner. I was born to walk the path of God; that was my heritage, my inheritance—not the garbage heap.

An amazing phenomenon occurred. Now that I saw the truth and desired it, the lie had no power. I told Ed, "In my spirit I see a pile of dirty clothes on the floor. They stink of fear and death. I used to wear them—but not anymore. How marvelous is God that He would reach into the garbage heap with His holy hands. As He picked me up those filthy rags fell off and were replaced with a beautiful white gown. My new princess dress is adorned with a royal blue sash which displays the King's name. This is what I'll now wear as I walk my path."

We both laughed with delight. "I love my new position, so how do I keep myself there and not go back to cowering in the corner?" I asked.

"Of course you wouldn't consciously go back to the corner, but it is familiar territory and walking the righteous path as an ambassador can feel awkward at times. The first step is knowing that you have a choice to either cower in the corner or walk the path. God opened your eyes to that, but in my spirit I still see that woman yelling at you causing you to fear."

Ed asked me to look up the verse about love casting out fear. After a quick search in my Bible software program, I read 1 John 4:18. "There is no fear in love; but perfect love casts out fear, because fear involves torment. But he who fears has not been made perfect in love."

Ed replied, "For your heart to be free of fear, you have to have perfect love toward God, and understand and accept the perfect love He has for you. To make room for His love, God has cleaned up the mess in your heart this past year. Unfortunately there's still fear there, which means you're not dwelling in perfect love yet."

I realized that as a child, I was corrected, scolded, and coerced with fear tactics. That taught me to live in fear. I was always afraid something bad would happen or that I might die.

Ed said, "The fear embedded into you caused you to detour off your God-designed path, and has kept you from having love perfected in you. Perfect love knows that if you died today, you would be with Jesus, and the fear of death is removed. That's when fear has no power."

I wondered how I could overcome the fear of death.

Ed said, "Remember, Satan can't kill you. He can kill your body—but that's not who you are. You're a spirit, and Satan can't kill your spirit. He can only try to keep you living in fear to prevent you from doing what God wants you to do—walk your path."

"I'm determined to stay on my path. But how do I find it within myself to walk it without fear and in perfect love toward God?" I asked.

"God's perfect love died for you, so you have to be willing to die for Him, that is allow the girl, the old you, to die. Then you won't return to hiding in that corner. For the girl to die, you have to fully trust God. To fully trust God, you'll need to know Him more intimately than you know fear.

To fully trust God, you'll need to know Him more intimately than you know fear.

"By the way, God does want you to have one fear: fear of the Lord. You're to reverence Him; respectfully honor who He is and His power. The fear of the Lord and perfect love are like interlaced fingers, separate yet equal, fitting perfectly together. If you walk your stepping stones in the fear of the Lord and your love for God is perfected, then fear can't penetrate your heart and you'll never crouch in the corner again."

 Butter Melts

And the Lord said "Simon, Simon! Indeed, Satan has asked for you,
that he may sift you as wheat."
—Luke 22:31

THE NEXT TWO WEEKS were a time of respite. Christmas came and went without much commotion. Hannah had some time off from school, and I had vacation from work. My sleep problems didn't improve, but the change in our schedule allowed extra time to sleep in the morning. Since I felt better, I started wondering why I didn't hear from God very much. I still desired more intimacy with Him. When Ed and I got together to pray, we asked God for insight.

"Let's look at Ephesians chapter two," Ed suggested. "And you He made alive, who were dead in trespasses and sins, in which you once walked according to the course of this world, according to the prince of the power of the air, the spirit who now works in the sons of disobedience, among whom also we all once conducted ourselves in the lusts of our flesh, fulfilling the desires of the flesh and of the mind, and were by nature children of wrath, just as the others" (v. 1-3).

Ed explained, "Before you were a child of God, you were in Satan's kingdom and unwittingly subjected yourself to him. He trained you in his ungodly ways. To clarify this I'll give you an example. When you were in Satan's kingdom, it was like you lived in Mongolia, but when God brought you into His kingdom you moved to California. At times you act like you live in Mongolia because you haven't completely assimilated to California yet. You need time to acclimate to the new culture; wear different clothes, speak a new language, and eat unfamiliar foods. Being a Christian involves the same concept; it takes time to adapt to God's kingdom."

"Continue with the next few verses in Ephesians," Ed instructed.

I read, "'But God, who is rich in mercy, because of His great love with which He loved us, even when we were dead in trespasses, made us alive together with Christ (by grace you have been saved), and raised us up together, and made us sit together in the heavenly places in Christ Jesus'" (Eph. 2:4-6).

Ed explained, "You were made alive with Christ, so it's impossible to be alive in Him and not be intimate with Him. God raised you up with Jesus and made you sit together in heavenly places, yet you struggle with this—how could little ole you sit with Jesus? You sit there because God made you sit together; He made a place for you at His table, and He gave you a seat. You're shoulder to shoulder with everyone else in the kingdom of Heaven and you're as intimate with Christ as anyone else at that table. Not because of what you've done or believed, but because of what God has done for you. He caused you to sit together with Him in heavenly places. He took you out of Mongolia and put you in California, but you don't fully understand all that has happened to you."

Ed came over to the computer and read Ephesians 2:10, "'For we are His workmanship, created in Christ Jesus for good works, which God prepared beforehand that we should walk in them.'"

I'd read this verse many times. However, I hadn't seen myself as *God's* workmanship. I always thought I was a product of my parents.

Ed continued, "Ephesians 2:13 goes on to say, 'But now in Christ Jesus, you who once were far off have been brought near by the blood of Christ.' You were once far from God, but the blood of Christ brought you near. He made a room for you in His mansion and set a place for you at His table. Being in Christ automatically puts you in a place of intimacy with God."

"I see my error." I said. "I've measured intimacy by how close I feel to God or how often I hear His voice. I thought the more He talks to me, the more intimate we are, and if I don't hear Him much, then we aren't very close."

"God wants to clarify this issue with you today. You can know Him better and trust and love Him more. He also wants you to realize that because of Christ, you're already as intimate with Him as you could ever be. You don't understand your true relationship with God because your knowledge of intimacy is based on feelings and interactions you've had with others. God wants these faulty ideas of intimacy to go by the wayside."

This was really sinking in to me.

After praying a few minutes, Ed looked up Luke 17:12-17. He read it out loud. "'Then as He entered a certain village, there met Him ten men who were lepers, who stood afar off. And they lifted up their voices and said, 'Jesus, Master, have mercy on us!' So when He saw them, He said to them, 'Go, show yourselves to the priests.' And so it was that as they went, they were cleansed. And one of them, when he saw that he was healed, returned, and with a loud voice glorified God, and fell down on his face at His feet, giving Him thanks. And he was a Samaritan. So Jesus answered and said, 'Were there not ten cleansed? But where are the nine?'"

Ed asked, "Have you ever prostrated yourself in front of God and thanked Him?"

"No. And as I'm thinking about it, it seems like a hard thing to do. But why?"

"As a little girl your heart was tender toward your dad, but that tenderness was trampled on and pain entered your heart. So as you grew up, you made a decision: you would protect your heart so your dad could never hurt you again. You carried your guarded heart into your relationship with your heavenly Father. Though you desire more intimacy with God, you come up against this wall you've built—and your desire cannot overcome your own mandate.

"And you made another life decision that you would never be grateful or thankful to your dad. Again, you unknowingly applied this to your Father God. You made these decisions when you lived in Mongolia and the culture warranted them. However, that way of life is unacceptable with a loving Father in California."

God's wisdom continued to come through Ed. "These decisions have severed lines of communication between God and you. They've created the same gaps in your relationship that exist between you and your dad. It's like you've put yourself on an island and built a moat around yourself. Your dad is on the other side of the moat—but now so is God. God wants to bridge the gap so you can have the close relationship with Him that you never had with your dad."

"I want to be closer to God," I replied.

"But whenever God rolls out the red carpet from His throne to your heart, you instinctively roll it back up to protect yourself. You've never known a father's love, so you don't have an example of father-daughter intimacy."

"What if I'm unable to know God's love?" I asked.

"You will. Your desire for God will act as a drawbridge, allowing Him to cross into forbidden territory. God will gently approach you, and beckon you, even entice you into a loving relationship with Him. Though He won't go beyond what you feel safe with. To slacken the drawbridge, to change your habit of self-protection, God wants you to kneel before Him and yield to His sovereignty."

Your desire for God will act as a drawbridge, allowing Him to cross into forbidden territory.

I got on my knees, closed my eyes, and lifted my hands to God. I quietly prayed in tongues while I envisioned myself on the red carpet before His throne. When I got up I didn't feel any different, but I had voluntarily submitted myself to God and His will.

Ed and I continued praying until he said, "You couldn't have true thankfulness in your heart toward God when He was on the other side of the moat. Do you remember a couple of months back when God asked you 'Where are you?' and it felt like an arrow pierced your heart?"

"Yes." I said.

"Your heart knew it wasn't thankful and hadn't worshiped at Jesus's feet. You were one of the nine. It wasn't out of rebellion or arrogance, but because your previous decision rendered you unable to have heartfelt thanks to God. Don't condemn yourself for this. Your lack of gratitude wasn't intentional; it was a result of conditioning."

The torturous nights of sleeplessness continued, and I became severely sleep deprived again. Ed and I came to God in prayer, asking Him for an answer to this ongoing problem.

Ed said, "I hear the word *authority*. Let's look at how you perceive authority again. As a child, you were taught that you had no authority. You were conditioned to submit to others. As an adult, you learned you have authority over yourself, but your prior training still declares you have no authority over others, which is why you have been so easily abused."

I agreed with Ed so far.

Ed continued, "God has given you *command authority* over the enemy, and He expects you to exercise it. You need to realize you have the same authority over the enemy that your dad used to have over you. Just as you had no option but to surrender to his authority, the devil and his demons have to concede to yours. They can't disregard it because they can't violate the Word of God.

"In my spirit I see a little girl. Three boys holding big sticks are running after her. They intend to beat her. It looks like she has no defense; she'll have to suffer the beating and hope to live through it. But wait. The girl turns and stomps her foot at them and commands them to go. They flee. She doesn't scare them away, they respond to her authority—they have to. That girl is you. God gave you His authority, and as Jesus sometimes got angry with His enemies, you have to oppose your enemy with the same righteous anger—not the unrighteous anger your dad used."

God's teachings on authority were changing my opinion of myself, but I wasn't hearing many demonic voices to command away. My biggest need was sleep, and I was becoming desperate. Ed and I had been praying a lot since this insomnia began, recently up to three times a week.

As we descended into our prayer room, Ed said, "I feel apprehensive today. Each time we pray, I assume God's revelations will resolve your sleeplessness, but they don't."

Even so, God was faithful and spoke to me through Ed again. I found out that my beliefs were wavering with my circumstances. While my mind knew my situation didn't alter God's love, my heart still linked my circumstances and performance to acceptance. It became clear to me that my picture of God still had to change. Rather than default to a negative view of God, I needed to be spring-loaded to see His love. I also had to accept that I couldn't make God change His mind about me, even when I made mistakes. I realized I did not have the power to change God's opinion or love for me based on my actions, thank goodness!

The word *unquenchable* came to Ed. I did a Bible word search and found it in Matthew 3:12. It says, "His winnowing fan is in His hand, and He will thoroughly clean out His threshing floor, and gather His wheat into the barn; but He will burn up the chaff with unquenchable fire."

Ed explained, "A husk, or hull, covers grain while it grows, but it has no value at harvest time so it's separated from the grain. It's then called chaff. You're the wheat, and God has gathered you to Himself. The destructive part of your childhood is the husk; it surrounded you as you grew, but it has no value, so God is removing it and burning the chaff in the fire."

Ed felt led by the Holy Spirit to anoint me with oil and pray for my thoughts. As Ed rubbed oil on my forehead, he said, "I pray that Denise can see the new raiment you have clothed her in, and she knows the dirty old garments are forever gone. I pray she realizes she lives in her robe of righteousness and she can't wear it out, can't wear it off, and can't stain it, because it's been put on her by you."

As Ed wiped the oil off his finger, he said, "Your heart needs to accept that God's love has clothed you in a robe of righteousness. It's done for you, it's not circumstantial or performance-based, and so you can't undo it."

We were done praying, and as Ed headed for the stairs, I told him, "I've been acutely aware of God's presence the last few days. I should be comforted; instead I feel nervous and unsure how to act. What if I say or do something He doesn't like? Should I talk to God or pretend I don't notice Him?"

Ed turned and said, "God is drawing close to you, but you're still defaulting to the preconditioned reaction you had with your dad—apprehension that something bad would happen. God is gently presenting Himself. You should turn your heart toward Him and respond like you do to any other pleasant person."

Next time, I will love God back. I'll tell God I love Him and thank Him for being close to me.

Even though progress was being made, my sleeplessness continued and the anxiety increased. I became very emotional and cried a lot. I cried in my car to and from work, I cried when Hannah and I played, and I cried in my bed at night. I didn't know how much longer I could go on like this.

One night, as I went through the motions of making dinner, Ed called to say he was coming over. A few minutes after he arrived, we started praying. He approached me and forcefully said, "You spirit of fear, you come out of her now. You come out now in Jesus name and don't come back. Get out, get out, GET OUT!"

My legs got weak and I sank to the floor. I trembled and then coughed. Then I started to cry. When I finished, I wiped my eyes with my shirt and stood up. I felt relieved and overwhelmingly thankful.

Ed calmly explained, "Earlier today, God told me there was a spirit of fear in you. He also confronted me about my reluctance to use my authority lately. God reassured me that if I had enough faith to be saved, then I had enough faith to cast out a demon.

"God also instructed me to read Mark 9:17-29, the account of Jesus commanding a foul spirit to come out of a boy. This spirit had entered the boy at an early age, and tormented him for years. The spirit didn't always manifest itself. Other times the evil spirit would throw the child into fire or water. This particular spirit was apparently of a stronger caliber, as the disciples couldn't command it to come out. In verse 29 Jesus said, 'This kind can come out by nothing but prayer and fasting.' God told me to fast for the day. This spirit must have had greater power than those we have dealt with so far."

Ed continued, "God also showed me an image of you and your sister playing with a Ouija board. Though you were a child at the time and didn't take the Ouija board seriously, you granted that spirit the right to come into you because you entered into Satan's realm—the occult. Like the spirit in Mark 9, this spirit interfered in your life, but it didn't manifest itself all the time. I sensed that spirit of fear leave when you trembled. I know it can't come back."

Now that the spirit of fear was gone I needed to be filled with God's peace. I initially planned to ask Ed to pray for me, but I recognized I was capable of doing this myself, so I simply asked God to fill me with His peace.

With my mind and body still running on fumes because of the ongoing insomnia, I began to doubt this was the end of the fight. A few days later Ed came over. I updated him on the status of my sleep and how I had felt the need to be filled with God's peace.

As we prayed, God's wisdom came through Ed. "This *feeling* you had was God speaking to you. He's sharpening your hearing skills so you won't need my help so often, and He wants you to hear His voice for yourself. To further improve your ability to hear God, a building block has to be removed—and it stems from your childhood church. At some point, you decided you didn't want what your church had to offer, and if they were people of God, then you didn't want God either. That decision put distance between God and you."

As Ed spoke, I realized that I heard God's voice at times, but it was usually faint and unfamiliar, making me wonder if it was actually Him. I was also under the impression that I would only hear from God on big issues.

Ed explained, "Your spirit knows God's voice, but your mind doesn't fully understand that He talks to you through your spirit. This past year, your mind has seen the mounting evidence that God frequently speaks to you. Now your mind has a hard lesson to learn: it can no longer be in charge. It has to submit to and be led by your spirit. Then your spirit can clearly hear God's voice and your mind will accept it is God. You also have to discard that old building block, the one that rejects what God has to offer."

For almost six weeks I had been meditating on Psalm 4:8 to help me sleep. I started by reciting the Psalm in my head and this calmed my mind down. Because of God's teachings on authority, I commanded (in Jesus name) my heart rate to slow down—and it did. That enabled my body to relax. Once my body settled down, I stopped repeating the verse and kept my mind blank. Shortly afterward, I fell asleep. I was excited about what I had accomplished, and over time it became easier and I was able to fall asleep faster. But my sleep was still far from peaceful; my body rebelled against me and woke me every one to two hours. I thought when the spirit of fear left, it would take my sleeping problems with it. It didn't, but it took away the fear attached to not being able to sleep, and that gave me some peace.

One night I was awakened when an object was thrown into my heart. I didn't fully wake up because I was in a deep sleep, but my spirit knew what happened, and it wasn't good. In my groggy state I uttered a groan, rolled over, and went back to sleep.

The next day Ed came over after dinner to pray. As we began to circle around the room, he said, "I want to tell you about a dream I had last night. I was in a dark room, though there was just enough light to see outlines. As I looked around the room I saw a witch. Its face was vividly white, and it had white hair. It knelt beside you as you lay in bed. I said "You!" to the witch, and it looked at me with a startled look, as though it had been caught doing something wrong. I didn't fear the witch. I actually pitied it because of what it had become."

I declared, "Your dream is triggering my memory. Something happened to me last night with a witch or witchcraft. It's too vague to remember though." As I tried to think of what happened, Ed told me that earlier in the day God gave him the word *terah*. He looked it up; it's Hebrew for wanderer or loiterer.

Together we discovered the connection. "That's the link!" Ed proclaimed. "The witch is a lingering spirit, a loiterer hanging around. The witch has no authority, yet it's violating God's will. All demons and witches violate God's will, but God doesn't stop them— He expects us to. That's why Jesus gave us authority over the enemy. We need to exercise it over that witch and her demonic assignment against you. But there's a problem. You're reluctant to use the authority Jesus gave you because you still see yourself as a servant rather than a commander."

I remained attentive while Ed explained my authority in a different way. "God gave humankind dominion, or authority, over the earth. When Adam and Eve disobeyed God, they submitted themselves to Satan. But Jesus came and led captivity captive (Eph. 4:8) and said, 'But be of good cheer, I have overcome the world' (John 16:33), the world that Satan is god of. You have authority over the "works" of the enemy, including that witch, because of the "work" Jesus did."

I told Ed that my reluctance had turned to willingness, but I didn't have much experience exercising God's authority.

Ed said, "When you graduated as a nurse practitioner you had your diploma, but you likely felt inept because you hadn't functioned in that role yet. Compare your first job with your practice now. With almost ten years of experience, you're much more knowledgeable and proficient. You only got the experience because you earned the degree, and you only earned the degree because you studied and trained. You have authority from God, which is your diploma signed with the blood of Jesus. Now you need to do what God has been training you to do.

"But," cautioned Ed, "First we need to consider that some people use the name of Jesus and don't have His authority."

Ed retrieved his phone from his shirt pocket and read for me the example in Acts 19:13-16. "Then some of the itinerant Jewish exorcists took it upon themselves to call the name of the Lord Jesus over those who had evil spirits, saying, "We exorcise you by the Jesus whom Paul preaches." Also there were seven sons of Sceva, a Jewish chief priest, who did so. And the evil spirit answered and said, "Jesus I know, and Paul I know; but who are you?" Then the man in whom the evil spirit was leaped on them, overpowered them, and prevailed against them so that they fled out of that house naked and wounded."

Ed continued, "These men couldn't just take Jesus's authority and apply it to the evil spirits; they had to be in Christ to exercise His authority. To be in Christ is to have a deep personal union with Him. This is possible only by the grace of God and being purified by the blood of Jesus. When this occurs, we have the authority of Jesus's name and the power of the Holy Spirit, and demons have to flee. The sons of Sceva commanded the demon to go, but it backfired because they weren't in Christ."

To be in Christ is to have a deep personal union with Him.

I said, "I know I'm in Christ, so I have the authority to command the witch to go. But I just feel so tired and weary. Will you do it for me?"

Ed agreed and then proclaimed, "You witch, I saw you. You stay away from Denise's bedroom, stay away from her house. I speak God's peace to this house, and I speak to you, witch, that you can't come in this house. You cannot trespass again."

Ed's English commands then converted to tongues; the sounds were full of power and authority. Then he confidently said, "You subtle laying-in-the-woods malingering spirit, you are cast out of this house. Never come back!"

Once again, I became hopeful my sleeplessness would end. I let out a heavy sigh as I sat at my desk to rest.

Ed said, "There's one more thing I need to tell you. When exercising authority over demons, your mind has to yield to your spirit because that's who God designated that activity to. The mind and the flesh don't have the authority. You still have to learn to live in your spirit where you can hear the voice of God, recognize the hand of God, and perceive the works of the enemy."

Will I ever be able to do this, I wondered?

The next morning on my drive to work, my spirit relayed information to my mind about the object thrown into my heart. From this transfer of knowledge, I learned it was a fireball, and it had three components: the fear of losing my salvation, the fear of not being able to take care of my daughter, and the third part was vague, it had something to do with my mother.

I assumed the witch Ed saw at my bedside was the one who threw the fireball in my heart. I didn't know why, perhaps to put fear back in me. Regardless, I wanted it out now—I didn't want to wait until Ed and I prayed again. While sitting at a stoplight, I commanded, "In Jesus name, you fireball get out of me!" I coughed, and saw what looked like a small puff of smoke come out of my mouth. Peace came over me. After I got home, I called Ed and told him what I had learned and done.

That night I had a dream; a dream so real I thought it actually happened. I got out of bed to go to the bathroom and I started to feel lightheaded. I was about to pass out, so I lay myself on the floor near the doorway between my bedroom and the hall. This allowed the blood to come back to my brain, and as I lay there, I had a mental conversation with God. I told Him that He knew I was alone with Hannah, and I asked Him to take care of her. I asked that she wouldn't wake up and find me on the floor. Then I decided I should get the phone to call for help. As I tried to move, I discovered a gray, rubbery arm held me down. It came from behind me, near my neck and face, and extended over my shoulder and chest. I grabbed it and tried to push it off, but it was too strong. While I wrestled with it, I discerned it wanted me to reject God and give up my salvation. I became desperate to get away, so I bit it. A piece came off in my mouth; it was sticky and repulsive. I spit it out. The arm withdrew, and I got up and walked to the bathroom—where I wanted to go in the first place. I woke up with a jolt. I was still in bed.

I didn't know what this dream meant, so when Ed and I prayed later in the week, I told him every detail and we asked God for insight.

Revelation knowledge came through Ed. "The devil used your parents to precondition you to accept abuse. When they verbally and emotionally assaulted you, you couldn't confront them, so you learned to be passive and take what you were given. Because of your past training you've tolerated the devil's abuse. You used to let the devil kick you around, but your character has started to change."

"That's right," I said. "After I learned about the fireball, I boldly told that weapon of the enemy to get out. I didn't wait for you; I stood against the devil myself."

Ed said, "In your dream, which was a spiritual manifestation of abuse by a demon, you fought back and that enabled you to get free and walk away. You didn't cower in the corner, but you opposed your abuser.

"I feel like God wants me to pray for your ears and anoint your earlobes with oil. Did you know that in ancient Israel, if a servant loved his master and didn't want to go free, the master would pierce his ear with an awl to mark them as a lifelong servant? (Exod. 21:5-6). This served as a contract or covenant between them. The master would provide the needs of the servant and the servant would forever give up his freedom to obediently do the will of his master. Putting oil on your physical ears is symbolic of your spiritual ears becoming permanently marked to hear the Holy Spirit and carry out the Master's Call."

As Ed put oil on my ears he prayed. "Lord, I ask that Denise's ears would be permanently marked to hear you because she has become a permanent slave to you, a servant to you. I pray she has ears to hear what the Spirit is saying to her. She will not turn to the left or to the right; she will continue to go toward the voice of her Master. The barrier, the barrier, the old habit of saying, 'I can't hear God' has to go; those thoughts have to yield to the Holy Spirit."

I told Ed that I felt encouraged that this inomnia nightmare might finally end. Regardless, I was excited that God had made me His permanent servant, and it gave me peace.

As we headed upstairs, Ed noticed the sun shone through the glass on my front door causing prisms of light on the carpet. He pointed it out to me and said, "There's blue, purple, orange, and yellow separated out, but if the colors were together, they would look like normal sunlight. This can be used to illustrate that God speaks in many different ways—His voice is like the rainbow of colors that are on the floor. You expect Him to always speak in the same way, with the color white, so when He speaks in a different color, you don't recognize His voice—that's why you needed your spiritual ears marked."

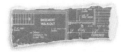

Ed developed some health problems and was admitted to the hospital. Doctors thought maybe his issues were due to stress, dehydration, or a virus. He fully recovered and was released after a couple of days. I partially blamed myself for his deteriorating health; we had prayed ten times this past month and usually two to three hours each time. I told myself and Ed that from now on, we would only pray once a week. I was not willing to jeopardize Ed's life to save my own.

In light of this, I asked God if I should take anti-anxiety medication to help my sleep situation. He gave me a word of wisdom; the woman who pestered the judge for justice. I had read this story before, but I didn't know it well. I found it in Luke 18:1-8, the parable of the persistent widow. In this parable Jesus reminded us to always pray and not lose heart. As I studied these verses, I learned that if I continued to go to God in prayer with desperate pleas, strong arguments, and loud cries, He would hear my cause, give me justice, and deliver me from my adversary.

I was encouraged, yet my sleep didn't improve. Within the week I started my left-over anti-anxiety pills hoping they would help. I was not the persistent widow; my attitude soured, my heart was heavy, and I didn't want to pray with Ed anymore. I just wanted to hide and forget about my life. The enemy spoke lies to me: *This isn't working* and *I can't keep going on like this.* I believed him. I yelled at God, "How much healing does my heart need? How many demons need to be cast out? How many lies need to be replaced with truths before this is resolved?!"

My frustration with the ups and downs of this journey allowed the devil's lies to flourish. I had triumph after triumph, yet deception came in because I expected this fight should have been over already. The devil couldn't take away God's promise of victory—unless he deceived me into quitting.

The devil couldn't take away God's promise of victory—unless he deceived me into quitting.

Ed knew I needed support, so he came to my house to pray for me. I was slumped on the couch, so he sat next to me and put his hand on my shoulder. "Lord, I pray that Denise will have your peace that surpasses understanding, that she'll have the ability to completely trust you in the midst of the fiery furnace. I ask you to show her the trust of the Father, of the One who never leaves her and meets her every need." Ed looked at me and said, "Your trust in God has been quietly altered. The devil is using lies to drive your confidence in God away."

"I know," I replied. "I've started to ask God, 'If you love me, then why are you allowing me to go through these never-ending battles?'"

"With all God has brought you through, you should be confident that God will help you overcome this."

I felt bad for doubting God. I broke down and sobbed, "I've lost patience with trying to find a cause and a solution to this sleep problem. I'm so tired of the roller coaster ride of good days and bad days."

As I sat on the couch crying, Ed encouraged me. "It's better to have a victory that lasts three days than no victory at all. All the victories you've had are true victories because you've grown through each battle."

Ed stood up and stared at the floor. "I see a blade of grass in my mind. The blade starts underground so it has to strive there. It struggles against the dirt's resistance before it will see the light. Like the blade of grass, you're pushing against the enemy's resistance, and in the process, you're being made stronger. Eventually, you'll come through the dirt into the fresh air and sunshine. Until then, you need to trust there will be an end to this, and that God is with you as you push through."

I always felt better after getting a word from God. I tried to keep a thankful attitude that I could still work and take care of Hannah, but as the sleepless nights continued, I grew hopeless. I was exhausted and confused about why this was happening. On the way home from work one day, I cried to God about my life. I thought things couldn't possibly get worse.

"Run your car off the freeway," the devil jeered at me.

"Shut up!" I yelled through my tears.

A year had passed since the night of the crisis, and I had run into a glass wall. I couldn't see the wall, but it was definitely there. Ed came over to pray, and we asked God why I was still being harassed. Why did every victory seem to lead to defeat?

After a few minutes of praying, Ed looked up a verse. "Psalm 91:3 says, 'Surely He shall deliver you from the snare of the fowler.' The fowler is a trapper. He constantly watches his prey and at the right time he pulls the trigger on the snare. The prey is not aware of the trap, and as it springs shut, it's captured."

"Your analogy points right to Satan," I told Ed.

"You're under attack and being ensnared because you're still not functioning in the full authority you've been deputized into. You can't fulfill that position because sometimes you act like a victim rather than the warrior you're supposed to be."

"Part of me doesn't want to fight. I think it's because my parents always fought, and I promised myself I wouldn't be like them," I replied.

Ed warned, "By making that decision you've inadvertently become a victim. Unless you want to become one of the devil's casualties, you'll have to fight back. Not as your parents taught you; you'll fight the good fight of faith (1 Tim. 6:12). To become a fighter, part of your character has to be rebuilt; it has to be broken down, melted, and reshaped."

Unless you want to become one of the devil's casualties, you'll have to fight back. Not as your parents taught you; you'll fight the good fight of faith.

That's the glass wall, I thought.

Learning the simple truth that this was a godly battle, and I wouldn't be fighting like my parents did, allowed me to give up the victim mentality and envision myself as a conquering soldier. That was the first step.

A week later, Ed came over to pray. "Earlier today God instructed me to study Mark 4:28. It says, 'For the earth yields crops by itself: first the blade, then the head, after that the full grain in the head.' This verse reminded me of the image of grass I saw in my mind last week. This time God showed me a detailed picture. I saw a seed of corn planted in a hole and dirt was stomped down on it. The dry seed in that dark place could come alive, although first it had to grow roots and then push itself through the dirt's resistance. When the fragile blades finally poked through the dirt, they were nourished by sunlight. As the plant absorbed water and light, it grew into a well-anchored stalk. Eventually full ears of corn, the fruit, came forth—all from a lifeless seed hidden in a dark place."

He continued, "God imprinted His plan in the seed and it could not be denied; the seed would become corn and nothing else. The seed's survival, growth, and ability to reproduce, all hinged on God's plan. That's a picture of you; relying on God's plan, and depending on the *Sonlight* to nourish and strengthen your faith and make you into the person you're supposed to be."

After a few minutes of praying, Ed said, "I keep hearing *stand* in my spirit. When we stand we don't go forward, but we don't quit or go back and undo what we've accomplished—those things were necessary to enable us to stand where we need to stand. We've used all our resources to push against the enemy's resistance."

"Now we have nothing left," I said softly.

"We can't take another step. We have to stand. Even though the devil's attack is aimed at you, we've battled this together. Now we've simultaneously come to the ends of ourselves."

I said, "This reminds me of the parable of the persistent widow; we have to keep pursuing God because only He can deliver me from my adversary. In our own power we can't do it, we have nothing left to fight with."

"Our swords and shields are bloodied and broken. Yet here we stand; we have not been defeated. Our only option now is to stand, and wait on the Deliverer."

I told Ed, "This past week, I've had two hours of broken sleep a night. My mind is foggy, and my body is weak from fatigue and filled with anxiety. I've been taking anti-anxiety medication for over a week and it hasn't helped. But through this ordeal, my trust and faith in God has grown to a new level."

Ed quoted Hebrews 10:38 which says, "The just shall live by faith."

I exclaimed, "I'm not only living by faith, my faith is all that's keeping me going. It's all I have left. I've learned to trust God day to day, and my faith has been sufficient just for the day at hand. I can't look at tomorrow; I focus only on the present. God has enabled me to live *today*, He didn't let me fail *today*, I functioned at work *today*, and I was able to be a mom *today*. Each day is truly a gift, no longer an empty cliché.

"I've acquired valuable skills in this valley of death. I've learned to genuinely praise God. I purposefully look for and thank Him for the good in each day; I'm alive and belong to Jesus, I still have my job, and my daughter is happy and safe. I've learned to keep my eyes on God, which helps me ignore the cries of my flesh. I've learned to take *every* thought captive—I can't afford not to.

"In this pit of darkness my faith has grown strong, but I feel like a puddle of melted butter. I've been opened up, dumped out, and I've melted on the floor. I'm a useless mess."

Ed replied, "Melted butter is a good analogy to explain the change taking place in you. Because of its structure, solid butter [the old man] has limited uses. When heat is applied [tribulations] the butter's structure weakens [yields control to God] and it becomes soft [humble]. Eventually its particles break free and the butter melts [a new creation]. The butter has kept its flavor, but now the Master Chef can use it in a greater variety of ways" [for His purpose and glory].

I wondered if God was going to come with a giant spoon and scoop me up. Would I be absorbed by His big sponge and squeezed out into a mold and shaped into something else?

Ed said, "Coming to the end of yourself allows you to become something new in Him."

Ed went on, "I'm not melted butter. I'm an empty gun. I feel like I've failed you, and have nothing left to offer, nothing to reload my gun with. We've reached our ends through different paths, but we have the same result. The knowledge that we can do nothing in our own strength has become a living reality.

Coming to the end of yourself allows you to become something new in Him.

"This is actually a place of victory. The past year has led us toward this; we fought this fight to do what God wanted us to do and learn what He wanted us to learn, but more importantly to get to the place He wants us to be. The prayers, the struggle and effort, the grief and tears all brought us here—where we have nothing left in us."

"I do feel strangely excited about this place," I said.

"Yes, because it's new territory. It's like we've washed up near an island after surviving a shipwreck. The storm, the fight with Satan, brought us closer to this island of emptiness with each successive wave of attack. We now walk knee-deep in calm water toward land. It's covered with thick, lush jungle and there are no paths. This environment is unfamiliar; we don't know what to do or how to live here. We'll have to completely rely on God in this place."

God could do something with us on the island that He couldn't do while we were in the storm. But we had just gotten out of the water, and needed to rest and warm ourselves in the "Son."

Leaving the Station

He who loves father or mother more than Me
is not worthy of Me.
—Matthew 10:37

THREE MONTHS HAD PASSED since my sleep problems began. I was supposed to be on the island of rest, but instead found myself still wading in the water, unable to reach that place of peace and respite.

Ed and I got together to pray. As we began, Ed said, "I feel like I'm walking through something thick, making it difficult to pray. We need to pray with more fervor today. I have a picture in my mind of toothpaste being squeezed out. We need to continue until the tube is empty."

We prayed loud and bold, until Ed started laughing. "I just envisioned the enemy being squirted with toothpaste! God wants you to lead now. I'll walk behind you, to support and lift you up in prayer."

I prayed ferociously, like an angry bear protecting her cub. I prayed until I couldn't catch my breath. When I finished, Ed said, "In my spirit I saw commands, demands, and instructions coming out of your mouth, and they manifested through your finger as you pointed at something I couldn't see. The resistance has left."

As we started to pray together again, we didn't know what to say to God. I told Ed, "I have no words; there's nothing left to say about my situation. God has done so much for me, and every time we pray He reveals secrets and mysteries to help me win this battle. The insights help for a while—until a new problem comes along. Now, I feel there's nothing to go on."

Ed said, "I sense that there's something about *nothing*. Would you describe again the fireball that witch threw into you? I suspect there's more to discover."

I described what I recalled. "It was one ball with three separate, yet interconnected components. One part was the fear of losing my salvation, another part was the fear I wouldn't be able to take care of Hannah, and the other part was vague. It had something to do with my mother. I commanded that fireball to get out of me. I assumed I was done with it."

Ed was silent for a moment and then said, "The *nothing* you feel is indeed something, and it seems connected to the fireball. Whatever it is, it's hidden itself. Because we can't see it, it looks as if nothing is there. Since we don't understand the portion of the fireball that has to do with your mother, let's focus our prayers on that."

After praying in tongues for a while, Ed said, "God has confirmed to me that *nothing* and *something about your mother* are connected, though He isn't telling me how."

I continued to pray, but Ed grew quiet. He came to me and put his hand on my shoulder. He commanded, "You come out of her you curse of mother, you curse called mother. You can't be in there, you have to let go. You have to leave, you curse called mother, come out!"

I was overcome by God's power; my legs got weak, and Ed laid me down on the floor. After a few minutes I was able to get up. I looked at Ed and said, "You were right on with what you spoke, however something odd happened. When I was on the floor, tears welled up and I wanted to cry, not because I was getting relief, but because I was in anguish. I felt an internal cry travel from my lower abdomen toward my head, and in the midst of that, I had a sensation of anxiety lifting off my chest. When I felt the anxiety leave, I had such relief that I got distracted from the painful cry that was also leaving my body. I'm not sure if the curse called mother came out, but the spirit of anxiety is gone. I feel lighter now!"

Ed remarked that my countenance changed too. He explained that when he became quiet, he was pressing into God for help. When he sensed God's presence, he waited on the Lord to fill him with His power. He let it build in him until he knew he had enough strength, that's when he cast the demon out. Ed said, "When I put my hand on your shoulder, I felt God's power moving in my spirit and I knew that demonic curse had to submit."

I was confident that the spirit of anxiety left me, yet I didn't see improvement with my sleep. I decided to stop taking the anti-anxiety medication because that didn't help either. I asked Ed to pray with me.

Ed read Isaiah 54:17 to me. "'No weapon formed against you shall prosper, and every tongue which rises against you in judgment You shall condemn. This is the heritage of the servants of the Lord, and their righteousness is from Me, says the Lord.' Denise, this assault is a weapon formed against you—with the intent to kill. But it can't prosper, and it can't kill you. Not because we're strong prayers or we command evil spirits, but because of your righteousness that comes from God."

As we began to pray, Ed said that he felt that resistance again and suggested we pray intensely. And we did.

When we finished, Ed said, "I heard you frequently say something like *ra-shan-yo* in tongues. My spirit liked it. Each time you said that word, the authority attached to it fought the resistance and defeated it. You led this particular battle because you exercised your authority in prayer. This was one of the few times so far that I've followed your lead."

I appreciated hearing that, but I had something else on my mind. I felt that we needed to pray in my bedroom because of the great heaviness I'd been feeling in there lately. We made our way in there to pray, waving to Hannah as we passed her room. After we prayed for a while, Ed told me, "When I walked in here, I felt like I'd walked into *nothing*. A feeling of *nothingness* was tangible to my spirit, and it was repulsive. I think the spirit of anxiety that left you has taken up residence in your room. It needs to go."

He turned his back to me and said, "You devil, you don't have permission to be here. In fact you are forbidden to be here. In the name of Jesus, you must leave. You can't reside here, you can't hide here."

Ed looked at me and told me to go in my walk-in closet and pray *ra-shan-yo* like I had done downstairs. He could tell I was hesitant, so he said, "Just pray in tongues with the authority of Christ in you and it will eventually come out." As I prayed, Ed interrupted with the great news that he sensed the evil spirit leave.

As we headed back downstairs to our regular prayer room, I remembered a conversation I had with my mom the night before. I told Ed that my mom and I were talking about how she often speaks negatively, and I said to my mom, "I used to have a mother who told me if you don't have something good to say, then don't say anything at all." When I said the word *mother,* I felt a yucky sensation in my spirit.

Ed advised me that I needed to understand my response to the word *mother.*

I inquired out loud, "Why did I say, 'I used to have a mother'? I don't normally talk like that. I should have said 'you used to tell me.' Also, I never refer to her as mother; I call her mom."

God's wisdom flowed through Ed and he explained it to me. "*Mother* launched a repulsive feeling in your spirit because you consider the word unrighteous. The term *mother* became distasteful in your childhood when you concluded your mom was unworthy of the respect that went with the definition of a mother. But there's more. God is telling me *subterfuge.* Let's revisit the night I commanded the curse of mother to come out of you."

I replied, "Yeah, I wasn't sure if the curse had left. It started to exit, but its release was aborted when I got distracted by the anxiety lifting off me."

"That's the subterfuge!" Ed exclaimed. "The spirit of anxiety sacrificed itself so the curse of mother could stay."

Ed wasted no time. He commanded, "You curse of mother, come out of her. You can't intertwine with her heart, and you can't cause brokenness in her heart. I pray for that broken heart and for the little girl who realized her mother abandoned her."

I didn't feel anything happen. Ed recommended that I write a letter to my mom, not to give to her, but as a means to express my feelings and to see what was in my heart.

"I've already done this with my dad. I'm not sure I want to go down that road again. But I am eager for this curse to be gone," I said.

Ed encouraged me to submit myself to God no matter how painful it became. "Beyond the agony, you'll find healing. Beyond the loss, you'll find restoration."

The next time Ed and I got together, I told him, "I've had a hard time talking to God recently. God doesn't feel distant, but rather I feel there is a barrier between us."

Ed reminded me of the unusually difficult task before me of getting rid of something that had been a big part of my life for many years. Ed explained that to help me accomplish this, God had turned my face away from Him and toward my mother—that was the barrier I felt.

I told Ed that I had followed his advice and written a letter to my mom. I didn't cry like I thought I would. As a matter of fact, the letter had an angry tone. As I wrote, I realized I had hated my mom as much as I had hated my dad. I was surprised I couldn't remember much detail of my relationship with her through the years.

Out of nowhere, Ed asked, "Is it more important to please God or to protect your mom?"

I hesitated. I was shocked at how difficult it was to answer the way I knew I should. I cared about my mom's happiness, but I didn't know I was protecting her.

Ed asked me to read my letter out loud.

I cleared my throat and read the opening sentences. "Dear Mom, Why did you let Dad do those mean things to me? Didn't you care how he treated me?"

As Ed and I talked about this, God opened my eyes to what I couldn't see before. My mom cared about me, yet not enough to change our situation. She knew my dad made our lives miserable, but even so, she stayed. For years she talked about divorcing him and often asked my opinion about it. I always hoped we would leave him. As time went on and we continued to stay, I grew angry at her for the choice she was making. She had gotten my hopes up for a better life and then crushed them over and over. My mom used to say, "You kids are all I have." I thought that meant she loved us, but now I saw that her focus was really on herself. She loved me when it met her needs and when it was good for her. Her love was utterly self-centered.

"As a mother, she was supposed to protect you, but she didn't," Ed said softly.

Ed was right, Mom knew that my dad's actions were harmful, yet due to her own fears, she didn't intervene when he verbally and emotionally abused me and the others. Her failure to defend me implied I wasn't worth putting herself at risk.

I gasped and looked at Ed. "Do you remember the image God gave me of my dad whipping me? My mom was the one who stood back and watched. I think over time I lost respect for her because of her cowardly behavior. She kept secrets and told lies to shelter me, really herself, from my dad."

Ed echoed, "As you were forced to live the lies she told, your roles reversed—you became responsible for protecting your mom from your dad. What else does your letter say?"

I read on, "You didn't take good care of your kids." I gazed at the floor and said to Ed, "What I meant to say is that Mom didn't take care of my need for love. When I was little, I wanted to be physically close to her, but my dad was jealous and shooed me away. She allowed my dad to dictate how much love she would give me. I didn't get the love I craved. Part of me died inside when my mom withheld her love and physical touch.

"As I grew older, Mom would sometimes try to hug me, but I would always pull away and say, 'Don't touch me.' It reminded me of my unfulfilled need for physical affection when I was young. Besides that, my mom and I had no conversations about my interests, my future, or who I was as a person. I heard only annoyance and disapproval in her tone, and many of her words demeaned me. As a teenager, I realized we didn't have a loving relationship, and I resigned that this was how it would always be. I buried my love for Mom and decided she could no longer be my mother. She failed her job, so in my heart, I fired her."

Ed said, "You've never forgiven your mom and more importantly, you've never asked God to forgive you for hating your mother. You need to do that today."

My heart felt ready, so I prayed, "Lord, I ask you to forgive me for hating my mom. And Mom, I forgive you for staying with Dad, even at my expense. I forgive you for putting your safety and comfort above mine. I forgive you for not defending me and for standing by as Dad abused me. I forgive you for each time you sent me away and didn't give me the love I needed. I forgive you for failing as a mother and for not truly loving me."

Ed said, "I sense that you've only scratched the surface. You are protecting the deeper layers because you still desire your mom's love. God has turned your face to look at your relationship with your mom, and though your mind accepts what you've learned, your heart is guarded. It doesn't want to admit these accusations against her are true."

He was right. I didn't want to deal with this issue. I just wanted God to take the junk out of my heart and put it straight in the trash!

Ed replied, "Unfortunately, God can't remove it until you see it and choose to let go of the heartache and hard feelings. But first you have to give Him permission to reveal the truth. What's more important; yielding to God or protecting your mom?"

Over the next week my sleep improved significantly, and I felt better than I had in months. I didn't know why my sleep changed, maybe because I forgave my mom, or perhaps the curse of mother was gone. Regardless, after three and a half months of torture I was ecstatic to have my life back.

One night I had a dream I could not stop thinking about. In the dream, my mom unexpectedly came to my house. As she stood on the front steps, she motioned for my dad to get out of the car and come in. I was angry she came over uninvited, but furious she told my dad to come in too. I yelled, "No! Don't let him in the door!" She did anyway. I was distraught; I didn't want them both at my house.

After I told this to Ed, he said, "I sense there is something significant about *them*. And I keep hearing *ashamed* in my spirit. Are you ashamed of your parents—ashamed of *them*?"

Yes. I was ashamed of how they looked, acted, and most of all how they talked to each other, especially in front of others. For some reason, I had taken responsibility for my parents' behavior, and I was concerned that people would look at them in a poor light and think badly of me. What I realized was that being ashamed was actually about me and not about my parents.

Ed received more revelation. "A dynamic occurs when you're with both of your parents that isn't present when you're with them individually. Alone with either one, you defend yourself, but when the three of you are together, you accuse yourself for this shameful component of your life—them—because you see yourself as their mirror reflection."

It was a lightbulb moment for me.

If I was a reflection of my parents, then that implied I was like them—which meant I was despicable. My sister confirmed this through the years with her degrading comment. She would often say, "You're just like mom." Ouch. Her words were like a knife in my heart. They reinforced that my conclusion was right and that I should continue to condemn myself.

Ed explained, "You didn't choose your parents, yet to escape your accuser, in this case you, you have to realize their unrighteousness is of themselves and not of you so that their ungodly actions and words can't cause you shame and self-condemnation. I have to ask you a simple question. Can you forgive yourself for having rotten parents?"

I prayed right then: "I forgive myself for having those parents. I forgive myself for the self-condemnation I allowed to grow in my heart. I forgive myself for being ashamed of myself because of them."

Ed prayed in tongues for a while. When he finished, he said, "God has given me an image of a lamprey eel. These eels attach themselves to fish by swimming alongside them until they get close enough to bite into their prey. The eel eats its way into the fish and sucks its blood to get nourishment. An eel is attached to you. This parasite isn't big enough to kill you, though it's getting its life from you and leaving you completely depleted."

Ed went on, "I want to pray for you, but I feel as if I'm stepping out on a limb with this one. All I know is something is deeply and firmly attached to you." He took my hand and forcefully prayed, "In the name of Jesus, you come out of her you viper, you life-sucking spirit. You can't stay. You're sucking into her heart and you cannot live there anymore. Get out, get out, GET OUT! In the name of Christ, let go. Your bonds are broken. Your power is broken!"

My ears burned and I felt woozy. I suddenly had a headache.

I finally felt like I had reached the island of rest. It was peaceful, but the quiet made me feel insecure in my relationship with God.

In our next prayer session, God spoke to me through Ed. "For over a year you've climbed mountains, gasped for air, begged for help, and learned to trust that God would rescue you. Now that the urgency of warfare is over, it's time to change how you approach God and make requests. You don't always have to come to God wearing your armor because peacetime calls for praise and thanks rather than fighting and desperate pleas for help.

"To survive the devil's attacks, you were forced to develop fighting and survival skills. Now that combat is over, you can't use your newly-acquired abilities, so you have a new crisis—lack of turmoil."

It was absolutely true. The peace I had longed for was now causing me distress. In the quiet I wondered where God was. I didn't have confidence that He was still with me. I trusted God in the midst of the storm, but not on the island. I didn't feel secure in His peace.

Ed explained, "This is all tied to your childhood. Most of the time your home had been a combat zone; you lived from crisis to crisis, and when there were times of peace, you anxiously awaited the next bomb to blow. That anticipation was almost as devastating as the explosions themselves. That's why you have a hard time relaxing in God's peace—you simply don't know how. Psalm 46:10 says, 'Be still, and know that I am God,' but you *God's peace is more powerful than any of His rescue missions.* don't know how to be still and trust God in the peace. To learn God's peace you'll have to spend time there. You'll have to understand that God's peace is more powerful than any of His rescue missions. You'll have to change your mindset from mighty soldier to beloved daughter resting in peace. You'll need to see that God is still God, in peacetime as well as in war."

In time I became more comfortable in God's peace, though I didn't spend all my time resting. God expected me to let Him finish the work He had begun. When Ed came over to pray one night, God revealed that something was still hidden. A spring-loaded trap lay along the wayside. As we talked about what it could be, I remembered my dream from the night before.

In my dream, I was an adult living with my parents. My mom began to scold me about religion. She told me I had to be Catholic because it was the only right way. She criticized the churches I had been to and said I hadn't learned the right things. I didn't yell back or defend myself, but I was angry that she berated me. I couldn't listen to her anymore, so I packed my suitcase and moved out.

Ed wasn't sure of the significance of the dream, but suggested we pray about *mother* as there seemed to be mysteries left unsolved. As we prayed I noticed something strange. My thumb was moving back and forth across the pads of my fingertips. It was as if my fingers were rolling over rosary beads. I told Ed that I had never prayed with a rosary, though I used to pray the Hail Mary which contained *Holy Mary Mother of God*.

Ed said, "In my spirit I see a freight train of several cars. Two distinct boxcars are joined together; one represents Mary Mother of God, and the other your mom. If we remove these two railcars of *mother* from the train, then they'll just sit on the tracks because they have no power of their own, and the train can move forward leaving them behind.

"Holy Mary Mother of God is echoing in my spirit. The words are overwhelming me and they are powerful—not in volume, but in importance. Mary Mother of God has to be disconnected from your mom because we aren't done with the curse of mother, and we can't continue to work on it when they're linked."

I wondered why we couldn't contend with the curse of mother if they were connected. This was all very mysterious.

Ed asked, "Is it possible for you to separate your mom from Mary Mother of God?"

I told Ed it would be hard to do because my mom was more committed to Mary than she was to Jesus. She elevated Mary above other mortals, believing that Mary influenced Jesus. I accepted that Mary gave birth to Jesus, although I refused the teachings that she was more than a humble girl, appointed to carry out a very important part of God's plan for humanity.

Ed replied, "You've rejected Mary as deity, but you don't want to reject your mom, so you've dragged along this other boxcar, Mary Mother of God.

"I hear *the unhooking* rumbling around in my spirit. I want to pray for the *mothers* to be separated." He prayed, "Thank you God, that in Denise's heart Mary Mother of God will be disconnected from her mother, that the authority of mother is broken and the illusion of the authority of mother can no longer stay."

Ed received more knowledge from God. "God designed mothers to be a blessing to their children. Unfortunately, Satan used your mom as a weapon against you. Your reaction to this was to decide your mom could no longer be your mother. Although you rejected this curse, you still want her love. You still want this blessed, God-designed relationship with your mom. It's natural to desire and pursue your mom's blessing, but you have to realize that you don't need it to feel complete. That's why the devil put *mother* in the fireball—because he could use it against you."

What Ed explained was true, but it was also true that God expected me to be a good daughter to my mom, even if she was unwilling or incapable of being a good mother, even if she had been a curse in my life. I wanted to be kind, helpful, and show love to my mom, and it would please God if I was a blessing to her. Luke 6:28 says, "Bless those who curse you."

As we walked up the stairs, Ed said, "The Mary Mother of God boxcar has been disconnected from your mom's boxcar. Oh, your dream. When you packed your things and left, you took all of your stuff, and nothing of your mom's—not even her beliefs about Mary. And another thing, if Satan can turn a blessing into a curse, God can certainly turn a curse into a blessing."

As I sat down on the couch to rest, five-year-old Hannah hopped on my lap to snuggle and get attention. Ed remarked, "Look at you two. Even though you're tired, Denise, you put your needs aside and give yourself to your daughter. That was a void in your life, wasn't it?"

When Hannah ran off to play, Ed asked, "Tell me again what happened the night I commanded the curse of mother to come out."

I recalled the incident. There was an internal, painful cry, like a wave of grief, leaving my body, but its momentum stopped when I got distracted by the external anxiety lifting off me.

Ed cried, "That grief is death! It still needs to come out!" He came and sat next to me and commanded, "Grief, you come out of her right now! You hidden, broken, spirit. You deep, heartbreaking hurt. You lifelong pain, come out! Oh my! The size of the handles on the box of grief you have is enormous! Thank you God, that you are the healer of the broken-hearted."

Ed likened this task to worming. When you try to pull a worm out of the ground, it does everything it can to pull away from you. As Ed exercised his God-given authority to remove this curse, it worked just as hard to pull itself back into the hole in my heart. It didn't want to let go, and Ed wasn't sure how to overpower its authority to hold on.

This time Ed stood up and said, "In the name of Jesus Christ, you come out of her now. You can't stay. In the name of Jesus get out, you're not welcome, you're not wanted, and you can't stay. Come out now, don't you hide; you have no right in her."

I continued to sit on the couch, but Ed walked around the living room, praying in tongues. After awhile he said, "God has revealed to me that the curse of mother didn't come through the fireball or a recently spoken word or phrase. It began when your mom was pregnant with you. Your dad didn't want another child, and when she told him the news of her pregnancy, he cursed your very existence. Your mom likely cried and grieved about her unwanted pregnancy and the problems it caused in her marriage."

I wondered if the grief that tried to leave my body was the same grief my mom had all those years ago. I wasn't sure if it was possible for my mom's grief to be passed onto me in the womb, but I knew the curse originated with my dad.

Ed said there was an important fact to be thankful for in all of this. Since I accepted Christ as my personal Savior, I did not carry the curse forward. For my daughter, Hannah, the term *mother* was a blessing—the way God designed it to be.

I tried to absorb what I'd learned about the fireball and the curse of mother. The fireball was from Satan, and thrown into me by the witch. Satan put *mother* in the fireball because he could somehow use it against me, likely because I still wanted my mom's love. When I learned of the fireball, I commanded it to come out, and it did.

The curse of mother did not come through the fireball; it came from my dad, through my mom, and into me when I was in my mother's womb. When Ed had attempted to cast the curse of mother out, it didn't go, and instead the spirit of anxiety sacrificed itself and left. When the curse had started to exit, it felt like a painful cry, a wave of grief. The grief was death; deep, heartbreaking hurt in my heart. Ed had commanded the grief to go, yet it clung tightly to me. We disconnected Mary Mother of God from my mom so we could continue to work on the curse of mother—that meant it wasn't gone yet. This was like untangling ancient snarls of twine from my body and soul.

During our next prayer time, God led us back to the boxcars. This time the two cars represented my mom and dad. In his spirit Ed saw these cars looked like old-time boxcars in a western movie. The wood was dark gray and weathered, and the metal parts were rusted. The outside showed no evidence of the destructive cargo they carried.

"It sounds as if there is nothing good about them. They're unattractive, rundown, and not at all useful," I said in dismay.

Ed replied, "These two boxcars contain your life with your parents and pictures of the old you. They're old dilapidated cars, and they carry all the events and memories you want to be free from. You and your parents' history together can't be changed, but you probably wouldn't look at them with disdain if they were filled with good things.

"The external condition of the boxcars doesn't matter. The content of the cars, either gold or manure, is what makes them desirable or undesirable. Your parents chose what went into the cars; they filled them with pieces of themselves, and the things they had done and said to you. This includes the curse of mother."

I thought all I could do was look back at their cars with disgust and wonder why they were still attached to me. But as the driver of my train, I decided what cars to pull, and though I couldn't change the content of their cars, I could disconnect them from the train. It was crucial that I disconnect them, then I could let go of my old relationships and build new ones—and more importantly, the curse would be gone.

Ed interpreted my tongues. "You just said *undoing* three different times. Remember, God gave us power and authority over the works of the enemy."

Was God saying we could undo a curse that started while I was in the womb? "How can we break a curse that began before I was born?" I asked Ed.

"God's power—his authority and ability—is not restricted by time. We'll break the curse off the same as if it came today. Some say the past can't be changed because the damage is done, but that's not true. Spiritual destruction can be undone. When you accepted Jesus, your spiritual condition changed from darkness to light, evil to holy, death to life."

God had turned my head so I could see that the curse still followed me and remove the curse-filled boxcars from the train, rather my life. God expected me to do this because I was the engineer, and my spirit was strong enough now to disconnect the cars myself.

I spoke to the curse. "God has exposed you, and I exercise the power and authority God has given me. I command that you are void, that you have no effect and that your power over me and my life is broken. You cannot follow me any longer. Get off my train and out of my life. I refuse you, I rebuke you, and I resist you. In the power of the name of Jesus you are broken from my life."

The boxcars were now disconnected and sidetracked in a desert someplace. As the engineer, I was still responsible for the cars, but they were no longer part of me. I would not pull them along. They could not hold me back!

The Great Physician

Then Jesus, moved with compassion, stretched out His hand and touched him, and said to him, "I am willing; be cleansed."
—Mark 1:41

I HAD LEARNED A LOT about my parents and the spiritual consequences of their actions. My dad had cursed me in the womb, and his performance-based philosophies had infiltrated my relationship with God. My mom loved me selfishly and put shame on me. They caused me to live in pain and fear, and shattered my self-worth. Strangely, I didn't have hard feelings toward my parents. They were broken and scarred themselves, and that's why they did what they did. They were just pawns of the devil.

My interactions with my parents hadn't change much from when this started, but I was different inside. Their words and behaviors didn't affect my heart like they used to, and my need for their love and acceptance diminished. I still loved and cared about them, but the suffering girl in my heart was breaking free from her bondage and getting ready to run.

One day, when I stood before my mirror and looked in my eyes, I saw a girl. She was young, attractive, and full of energy—I really liked her. She looked confident and happy and seemed to have no cares, like I would be if I were in Heaven. At my next prayer time with Ed, I told him about the girl I saw inside myself, and we prayed together about her.

Revelation came forth. Ed said, "The girl you saw in the mirror is the real you. She is without sin, shame, or guilt before God. You called her a girl rather than a woman because a girl is more like a daughter and that's how you're starting to see yourself—as God's daughter."

I wondered if this girl was who I should've been or who I was becoming. Perhaps they were one in the same?

Ed said, "This open-eyed vision you had was not an illusion. God removed the scales from your eyes and you saw your true self, your inheritance as God's daughter. God designed you as the girl in the mirror. You really are that girl, but you don't know that because the devil stole your identity when you were young. He disguised the guiltless, confident girl by dressing you as a rebellious, shameful, broken-hearted nobody."

God had been removing layer after layer of lies from my heart. He was unveiling who He created me to be.

God had been removing layer after layer of lies from my heart. He was unveiling who He created me to be. Ed looked up a verse and read Romans 12:2. "And do not be conformed to this world, but be transformed by the renewing of your mind, that you may prove what is that good and acceptable and perfect will of God." He said, "Your battle has been and will continue to be against the person that the devil, your parents, and the world turned you into. To win this fight, it's imperative that you keep renewing your mind until it lines up with the real you—the girl in the mirror."

After a moment of silence, Ed said, "God has given me a scenario to illustrate why you haven't lived as the girl in the mirror. Imagine that God owns a factory. When you came into the factory as a newborn baby, you were perfectly designed by God. He had drafted your blueprint and stamped it on your spirit before you were born. The factory had a production line just for you, and you were handed over to the workers. The owner (God) gave them the responsibility to make you into who you were supposed to be. Although many people worked on you throughout the assembly process, your parents, because of their position, had the greatest influence on your outcome. They all assembled you in the manner that seemed right to them, and they engraved *their* trademark on you. They did not produce you according to God's blueprint."

Ed continued, "When you became an adult, God appointed you as the production manager. As the manager you're required to examine the product they made, disassemble parts and revise them if needed, and if necessary fire the workers. But whenever you try to go onto the factory floor, you face an impassable sink hole. It looks like a bottomless pit and it stops you every time. I'm here to tell you that the pit is just a mirage. The enemy created it to stop you from going into the factory and correcting the problems, thereby preventing you from your original design and purpose."

I understood that God expected me to be who He created, but I didn't know how, as I still had features that didn't match the blueprint. Things in my soul didn't resemble the girl in the mirror. I had old ways of thinking, and the residue of old habits needed to be wiped away. Ed told me that I couldn't just look at the blueprint and figure out what needed repair; this was a spiritual work, not a logical exercise.

I said to Ed, "Okay, continuing with the factory analogy, I understand that the workers in charge of me didn't have the ability to correctly assemble me, and the product they built turned out vastly different from God's blueprint. I don't know how to fix over forty years of damage from multiple assembly line workers. I think the Creator should make the corrections."

Ed replied, "You have to do it. While you can't go to their workstations and make them undo what they've done, you can reshape or take out the malfunctioning parts and replace them with the correct pieces. In other words, do away with the old man and put on the new—which is actually the original design."

Ed looked up Ephesians 4:22-24 and read it to me. "That you put off, concerning your former conduct, the old man which grows corrupt according to the deceitful lusts and be renewed in the spirit of your mind, and that you put on the new man which was created according to God, in true righteousness and holiness."

As Ed and I discussed this, I learned that I can't simultaneously be the person Satan molded me into and the girl God created me to be. To live as the girl in the mirror, I had to allow God to show me what still needed to be fixed. If I decided to make the remaining changes, then I could use the Designer's assembly instructions, the Bible, to rebuild myself. Like everyone else, I was a work in progress.

I went through a lull where I felt that God was being silent in my life, so I tried to figure out if I had done something wrong. When Ed and I got together to pray, I told him how I felt and that I was open to correction from God if I needed it.

Ed replied, "Something's wrong about you being *open to correction*. Although you haven't done anything to upset God necessarily, your heart believes you're guilty. It concludes that God is quiet because you've done something wrong. This is an old habit sneaking out; you automatically assume you are guilty and condemn yourself. The blame you feel in your heart is real, only it's not true. You need to trust God, and not only trust Him, but love Him as well."

I did love God—with all my heart. Even so, I still hadn't learned how to have a conversation with Him that wasn't crisis-based. I knew how to talk to God as my rescuer, but not to God as Father. When I talked to God, it seemed formal and lacking intimacy. I had developed intimacy with Jesus my Savior, the Holy Spirit my teacher, and with God Almighty, but not with God as my Father. I didn't yet know how to be intimate with the Father—how to be His little girl.

Ed comforted, "Don't worry. It's because you weren't allowed to be a daughter to your dad. God will teach you how to be His daughter and have intimate communication with Him. That's part of the Father's role. You just have to let God love you and resolve to love Him back."

God had already shown me His love. He rescued me, protected me, healed my heart, and taught me about Himself. God proved His love during the most difficult time of my life. He never pushed me too hard or too far because He wasn't going to allow me to fail. At times I thought I failed God, but that was because as a child, I had been taught to see myself as a failure.

Ed said, "It's not up to you to decide. You are not your own judge—God is. He determines if you fail, and He won't permit you to fail. You *cannot* fail with Him. God's love is bigger than that!

You cannot fail with Him. God's love is bigger than that!

"The word *compassion* just came into my spirit. Compassion means you feel badly for someone and you want to help them because it hurts you to see them hurting; you feel their pain. God as your Father has great compassion and He wants you to know that He has compassion for you—for you personally."

I knew that God was filled with compassion, but I never thought about Him having compassion for me as an individual. It was hard to hear that He did.

"You resist this because you have a double standard; you have a lot of compassion for others, yet you won't accept it for yourself. You won't receive it because opening the door to your heart makes you feel vulnerable."

As I examined my recent battles and my life, I saw that compassion is who God is and what He does. It was compassion that sent Jesus as a sacrifice for our sins. And it was compassion that rescued me from my struggles. If I didn't accept God's compassion, then I couldn't accept His love or mercy, because they were all intertwined. I realized receiving God's compassion was a good thing. I lifted my face toward Heaven and said, "Lord, I freely accept your compassion."

"Now I hear the word *forbidden*," Ed said. "Not only were you not allowed to be a daughter to your dad, your dad actually forbade you to be his daughter. God does not forbid you to be His daughter; He accepts and approves you in Christ. And as His daughter, you are welcomed with open arms."

Being forbidden was like a rope wrapped around my heart; it held me captive to the condemnation of being a daughter. Rather than hastily cut the rope and cause me harm, God was unweaving the individual fibers to gradually loosen it. As He untied the lies of my identity, He was setting my captive heart free—making it free to love Him as a daughter should.

A few nights later I read a story out of a devotional book. It was about Naaman, the leprous commander of the Syrian army (2 Kings 5:1-19). When I read, "When Naaman believed and obeyed, God healed him," the words jumped off the page. I studied this further in my Bible and learned much about Naaman and God's mighty power to heal. I identified myself with Naaman. We were both courageous warriors, and we both had dishonorable afflictions.

As He untied the lies of my identity, He was setting my captive heart free—making it free to love Him as a daughter should.

As I examined the Scriptures further, I realized there were two parts to Naaman's healing. His flesh would be restored, and he would be clean (2 Kings 5:10). Not only would his leprosy be cured and his shame taken away, but he would be morally clean—pure and holy.

I was astounded that God wanted to pour out His love and compassion and heal my disease. For two days I was in a state of shock as my mind tried to grasp what God had revealed to my spirit. I was dumbstruck and couldn't talk to God, yet in this quiet time intimacy developed between us. I had the privilege of touching the edge of His loving-kindness. It was more powerful than any miracle He would do to heal me.

As I waited for God to heal me, the devil started another assault. I began to hear voices. They were negative comments about God and suggestions that I hurt myself in ridiculous ways such as gouging my eyes out. There were also quiet voices that I couldn't clearly understand. The external voices progressed to internal thoughts, and even though I had experienced deep intimacy with God a few days ago, I wondered if He still loved me or was mad at me. I felt unhappy and discouraged. After a few days of this, I updated Ed and asked him to pray with me.

As our session began, Ed said, "I hear the words *don't take it personally*. The devil's lies affect your heart because you let them in— you take them personally. When voices or thoughts come, you can't automatically allow them in, you have to take every thought captive to the obedience of Christ by pushing it through the filter that is Christ, and if it doesn't fit through the filter, it can't come in."

Push every thought through the filter that is Christ, and if it doesn't fit through the filter, it can't come in.

I thanked God for the reminder and then Ed prayed, "Thank you Lord that the gifts of the Spirit come through us, both of us. Oh no! As I said that, I saw a vision of a big saber-like sword come down and cut off my prayer. The sword was meant for you, but it didn't attack your person. It was trying to cut off the very path you are walking on. The sword was violent and powerful. It intends to forbid you from operating in the gifts of the Spirit. In reality it has absolutely no power to stop you."

Did this sword also intend to sever my path of faith for healing? I still believed God was going to heal me, and I was ready to receive it.

I told Ed, "I'm just waiting for my instructions. I assume since Naaman had to dip in the Jordan seven times, God is going to require an act of obedience from me."

Ed replied, "Let's examine the account of Peter walking on water. It starts with Jesus's disciples sailing across the sea, then the god of this world came against them with a storm. Satan used wave after wave to keep them from where they were supposed to go. Then Jesus came. Matthew 14:27-29 says, 'But immediately Jesus spoke to them, saying, "Be of good cheer! It is I; do not be afraid." And Peter answered Him and said, "Lord, if it is You, command me to come to You on the water." So He said, "Come." And when Peter had come down out of the boat, he walked on the water to go to Jesus.'"

I listened and thought *That's me! Lord, if you want to heal me, I'll do whatever you tell me to do.*

Ed continued, "Peter left his logic behind and got out of his place of safety. He was able to walk on the water until Satan told him the wind was too strong and the waves were too high. He took the devil's comments personally, and his faith was cut off by fear. He started to sink. The miracle was gone."

Ed looked me in the eyes. "Jesus still wants His disciples to function in faith. He wants us to get beyond our circumstances and safety and step out of the boat—believe in Him above everything else. God is using the story of Naaman to teach you a lesson in water walking. You have to take what God has shown you and elevate it above your circumstances. Your faith in healing has to be greater than the physical evidence in your body."

Both Peter and Naaman had to apply their faith, and they did that through obedience. Peter stepped out of the boat, and Naaman washed in the Jordan. Even though I understood this, I had received no command or instruction. Ed suggested that perhaps my act of obedience was to wait on God in faith, nothing more.

Ed called me the following day. "All day God has been telling me, 'I showed you the sword.' We didn't do anything about the sword! I need to come over to pray that through with you."

As we walked around, we recapped from the day before. We knew the sword was meant to stop me from walking on my God-given path; either operating in the gifts of the Spirit or receiving healing, or both. We didn't know what got cut off, the actual path or my ability to walk it.

"I want to reexamine the sword," Ed said. "It was violent—swift and powerful. The sword wasn't just an action; it also spoke a *no* command. Usually the devil comes against you with subtlety and deceit; this violent aspect is new. The violence isn't against you; it's directed at your walk with God. The enemy has been forced to escalate his tactics because he knows he's losing the battle. It's time for you to act though. You don't have to obey the *no* command. You can use your authority and rebuke it with a declaration of faith."

With determination in my voice, I said, "No weapon formed against me will prosper. This is the Word of God and I declare it over my life and over the path God has laid out for me. No sword can cut me off. No weapon of the enemy can prevent me from going where God wants me to go!"

When I finished, my body was tingling all over! Ed sensed my declaration of faith was actually a powerful declaration of war against the enemy of faith.

Ed said, "I see an image of a doorway. It represents a secret passage the devil uses to sneak into your life. This doorway was constructed when you were a child, and it has become an invisible part of you. The hidden passageway is your faith in the wrong things. Most of the time, your faith in God is strong. But occasionally, and recently, you slip back into deliberations with the enemy about God's love for you, your identity in Christ, or other topics he brings before you. When you entertain the devil's lies, or worse yet, take them personally, the door opens and allows the devil to come in and have his way."

As God reminded me yesterday, I couldn't automatically allow thoughts to come in. I had to analyze them, and take them captive if needed. This wasn't just a mental exercise, it was a spiritual battle. Ephesians 6:11 tells us to put on the whole armor of God so we can stand against the wiles of devil. This armor of truth, righteousness, peace, faith, salvation, and the Word of God were my weapons. In this situation I needed to raise my shield of faith when the enemy knocked at the door. This spiritual battle required spiritual weapons.

This spiritual battle required spiritual weapons.

As our time ended, I asked Ed, "Will you pray for my left arm? I know it seems random, but my collar bone started to hurt while we were praying today. I can barely move my arm."

Ed took my hand in his and said, "Thank you Lord for healing Denise's collar bone. I thank you that no spiritual weapon formed against her body will have any prosperity. Thank you that she can raise her...oh....that's her shield arm isn't it? Yes, thank you Lord, that the enemy can't hold her arm down and stop her from using her shield of faith."

Ed let go of my hand and turned to me. "Did you get that? You're right-handed, aren't you? That means you carry your sword in your right hand and your shield in your left. That pain is a physical manifestation of the enemy trying to hold down your shield of faith. I trust it is better now."

Two weeks had passed since God revealed His desire to heal me. I was experiencing an increasing amount of neck pain the last few months. I knew it was serious and required more than x-rays and physical therapy. I asked God to heal my neck, rather than the "leprosy," as the pain plagued me daily, and I believed surgery was needed.

As I waited for God to heal me, I found myself with a lot of questions about healing and faith. How would I know when I had enough faith to be healed? Or would God heal me out of compassion no matter my faith? Was I required to be obedient like Naaman? If so, I didn't know the next step.

During my Bible time, I was reading in the book of Philippians. A certain verse stood out to me. It said, "And be found in Him, not having my own righteousness, which is from the law, but that which is through faith in Christ, the righteousness which is from God by faith"(3:9). I saw that everything I knew to be true had come through faith; faith that I was accepted in the Beloved, that my name was written in the Lamb's Book of Life, and that God was leading me down His path—I needed faith to receive everything the Bible says.

I had proof of my faith. After I accepted Jesus as my Savior, I changed. I became generous and had a sudden distaste for alcohol and movies. My faith came first, but evidence followed, and the evidence reinforced my faith and gave me the ability to have more faith. God was telling me that faith for healing was no different than having faith in my right standing with Him—or any other Bible truth.

I continued to have faith for what God had shown me. I spoke His promises in faith, believing He would heal me. That's all I could do. There was no demon to defeat. Instead God was requiring me to grow.

After another week without being healed, I quit actively pursuing it. I wasn't going to stop believing for it, but I didn't want to pray about it anymore. If God wanted to heal me, then He would. Healing wasn't my priority, God was, and I wanted to pursue Him.

I hadn't sought healing in the first place. God initiated this when He spoke to me through the devotional book and led me to study Naaman's story. Though it would be great to be healed, I was more moved by God's love and compassion than any healing I might receive. Lack of healing would not change my relationship with God.

Healing wasn't my priority, God was, and I wanted to pursue Him.

Two nights later I was praying, talking to God about nothing in particular, and all of a sudden, I was struck with a bolt of lightning. Well, it wasn't real lightning, but it felt like it. For two seconds, I had excruciating pain pulsing through my cervical spine. I froze in my tracks as I was reeling from what had just happened. I feared I might be paralyzed. As I recovered from the pain and replayed the experience in my mind, I realized it didn't feel like the external manipulation of a spine adjustment. It was an internal realignment—a powerful work done inside my spinal canal. I moved my neck in all directions. I had no pain! God had performed a miracle. My neck was healed!

Not only did God heal me, but He honored my request and healed my neck. I remembered Romans 4:21 which says, "And being fully convinced that what He had promised, He was also able to perform." I thanked and praised God for His love and compassion, and for performing a healing miracle.

Life was good. The enemy's attacks had diminished, my sleep was peaceful, and God had healed my neck. As the assaults lessoned, God's involvement in my life was less evident. I didn't want my supernatural time with God to stop. When Ed came over to pray, I told him how I felt and asked, "Why do I need fireworks all the time?"

Ed knew my question was inspired by the Holy Spirit and we needed to explore it. After some thought, I said, "I desire supernatural events because I associate them with God working in me. Now that there are fewer fireworks, I feel as if my life-changing experiences are ending and I don't want them to."

Ed cautioned, "God doesn't operate only through fireworks. He also works through His loving-kindness, and you've already experienced change through His intimate nature."

As we prayed, I saw myself on a path and I explained it to Ed. "Off the right side of the path, there's a trail that leads to a fair. There are rides and games, and of course fireworks. On the left, a trail heads to a secluded beach bordered by soft swishing waves. I love both the fair and the beach. When the fireworks explode I get dramatic attention from God. My adrenaline is quenched at the intimate beach. Both satisfy. But most of my life is spent on the path itself. I hate the path. It seems like God ignores me there, and I see it as a place of stagnation."

Ed said, "You despise it because you see it as a lifeless dirt road. But God requires you to live on the path, and He wants you to know it's a good place where you can have as much of Him there as you do at the fair or the beach."

I told Ed I didn't know what to do with myself on the path. I felt like I was either waiting for the fireworks to start or longing for the soothing intimacy of the beach. Ed said, "The fair and the beach are distractions—from you. You forget about yourself when you watch the colors erupt or gaze at the water, and you know God is with you. You don't see God on the path. You just see yourself and that's why you don't like it. You don't see yourself as the girl in the mirror there. You only feel like her at the fair and at the beach."

I thought seeing myself as the girl in the mirror two out of three places was pretty good. The truth is, our lives are mostly lived on the path. The fair and the beach are extra blessings. However, there are also blessings on the path.

Ed said, "You can't perceive God on that dusty, dead road because He's not there. And neither are you. Close your eyes and take a close look at your path."

The fair and the beach are extra blessings. However, there are also blessings on the path.

I closed my eyes and saw lush, green grass with a few small, white flowers scattered throughout. Jesus was with me. Birds were chirping nearby. While it wasn't as fun as the fair or as peaceful as the beach, it wasn't the dead road I thought it was either. All of a sudden I felt happy, and I heard myself say, "I would like to live here."

Ed laughed.

As we ended our prayer time, Ed and I talked about God's work in healing my neck. Ed said, "Do you realize that you were on the path when God healed you?" I just smiled and shook my head. I had undeniable evidence that my Father was with me in the middle of the road.

It took some time to acclimate to my "new" path. I wasn't seeing fire-works or having intimate nights at the beach. I enjoyed this time, but again I wasn't hearing from God as much as I thought I should, so I called Ed and asked him to pray with me about this.

After we got into our usual prayer formation, God's wisdom came through Ed. "Your receptors, your ability to hear God's voice clearly, are turned off. Once again this is tied to your dad. Most things your dad said to you were negative, so to preserve yourself, you de-cided to tune him out, turn your receptors off to him. Your ears heard his words, yet your mind didn't acknowledge them. Because you er-roneously viewed God like your dad, you inadvertently turned off your receptors to God as well.

"In my spirit I see a bowtie around your neck. Over time the knot got tighter and tighter, until you couldn't take anything in. The bowtie is symbolic of your hearing receptors—they're tied in a knot."

"How can the knot be untied?" I asked.

"Deuteronomy 30:19 says 'I call heaven and earth as witnesses today against you, that I have set before you life and death, blessing and cursing; therefore choose life, that both you and your descendants may live.' You chose to turn off your receptors, so you can choose to turn them back on. Your dad spoke words of death, so it was logical to turn your receptors off. Your heavenly Father speaks words of life and you want to hear His voice, but you can't get beyond this child-hood decision—until now—it had to be exposed."

One of my favorite verses is, "You shall know the truth, and the truth shall make you free" (John 8:32). Once again, God's light had uncovered the truth in my life. Satan had used my relationship with my dad to precondition me to tune God out. But I decided to turn my receptors *on* to God! The knot was untied!

Casting Crowns

Fear not, for I am with you; be not dismayed, for I am your God.
I will strengthen you, Yes, I will help you,
I will uphold you with My righteous right hand.
—Isaiah 41:10

HANNAH BROUGHT HOME A BIBLE VERSE from school to memorize. It was John 15:14; "You are My friends if you do whatever I command you." She left the Scripture on the table where, during dinner, it seemed to stare at me. The next time Ed and I prayed together, I told him about it. He replied, "Our relationship with Jesus should progress from Savior to King to Commander to Friend."

"What's the difference between Jesus as King and Jesus as Commander?" I asked.

"As King, Jesus sits on the throne in a robe of righteousness giving orders to His servants. As Commander, Jesus is in the trenches with a sword in His hand, leading His soldiers into battle. Many believers try to advance their relationship with Jesus directly from Savior to Friend, but King and Commander can't be bypassed because Jesus established a sequence. In John 15:15 Jesus said, 'No longer do I call you servants, for a servant does not know what his master is doing; but I have called you friends.' *No longer servant* means that being a servant has to take place before friendship can occur."

For years I had thought of Jesus only as my Savior. When He told me to adopt Hannah, I followed His orders, but I didn't really regard Him as King. As I've gone through these battles, Jesus became my King and Commander. "Is Jesus supposed to become my friend now?" I inquired.

Ed replied, "Servants don't choose the King as their friend, or tell the King who His friends are—the King chooses His own friends. He selects those He trusts; servants who have proved themselves by being diligent and obedient. Servants only become friends if they demonstrate their allegiance. Yes, your King is asking you to become His friend. He's offering you His friendship because you've demonstrated your commitment to Him."

Just thinking about being a friend of Jesus made me nervous. It's different than being a daughter of God. I was afraid to be Jesus's friend because then I would be more vulnerable to Him. I trusted Jesus as King and Commander, but being an intimate friend would require more trust than sheer obedience to a higher authority.

Ed said, "You're apprehensive because Satan taught you to fear being close to God. As a child, you learned God was angry with you and hated you, so it was safer to keep your distance. Or better yet, try to hide from Him. Then maybe He would forget about you and you wouldn't get punished."

I knew in my mind that Jesus could be trusted. I wanted our relationship to progress.

Ed said, "Those lies in your heart still have power. To end their influence, you have to reject them."

Without a moment's hesitation, I said, "I refuse those lies. God is not scary or intimidating and it's better to be close to Him. Lord Jesus, I consider it an honor and a privilege to be your friend, and I gladly accept your offer of friendship."

"There's one more thing," Ed added. "Jesus's roles as King, Commander, and Friend will fluctuate. At times He'll give you orders, stand with you in battle, and converse or spend time with you as you go through life. Sometimes the roles will overlap, and the boundary lines will be difficult, if not impossible, to discern. This is a gray area. Friends are usually on the same level, but you're subordinate to your Friend Jesus, and if He wants you to do something, you're required to obey Him because He's still your King."

Later that night I tried to absorb the magnitude of being chosen as Jesus's friend. I felt blessed beyond measure. I tried to talk to Jesus as friend, but I was speechless. I just sat on the couch enjoying His presence. Our time was intimate and peaceful—like close friends spending time together, not needing to say a word.

Almost two years had passed since the night of the crisis. I wanted to do things for God in addition to seeking Him and nourishing our relationship. I told Ed, "I feel as if I'm in a work mode now."

Ed said, "We need to pray about that word *work*. We know that salvation is not attainable by works. Ephesians 2:8-9 says, 'For by grace you have been saved through faith, and that not of yourselves; it is the gift of God not of works, lest anyone should boast.' But we also know we have to put forth effort as we live our new life, as Philippians 2:12

says: 'Therefore, my beloved, as you have always obeyed, not as in my presence only, but now much more in my absence, work out your own salvation with fear and trembling.'"

I was initially surprised by the direction God was taking me. Though I had to admit that I had jumped back on the performance wheel, feeling concerned about the permanence of my salvation. I thought if I increased the amount of time I prayed and read my Bible, my salvation would be more secure.

It was so easy for me to fall back into believing the enemy's lie of performance-based acceptance. This belief was so ingrained in me that I was trying to improve my performance rather than live by the knowledge God had given me. I thought I needed to perform with increased Bible study and prayer in order to prevent being pulled away again. That wasn't the only reason I prayed and read my Bible, but in the back of my mind I knew it was crucial that I spend time with God. "If the enemy could pull me away once, I could be pulled away again," I told Ed.

> *Your reason for spending time with God should be to learn more about Him and walk closer with Him, not because you fear the enemy.*

Ed agreed, "If you stop praying and studying the Bible, you might get pulled away, because you need to keep yourself built up, as we all do. Your reason for spending time with God should be to learn more about Him and walk closer with Him, not because you fear the enemy. That's an important difference. Your motive is misdirected."

"But I have knowledge about Satan that most people don't have," I protested. "How can I disregard that information so my actions can be pure?"

"You don't need to forget what you've learned; you just need to understand how the devil has twisted your perspective. Once again, this stems from your childhood."

I could see that my parents had conditioned me to work (perform) in order to avoid harm. When that training surfaced, I started working to prevent the devil from pulling me away. As I tried to prevent an act of Satan, I turned my face toward him. If I worked out my salvation instead, then my face would be pointed toward God, and I wouldn't need to defend myself against the enemy. God was my best defense.

A couple of weeks later I was talking to my mom on the phone. For some reason she said, "Shame on you." My body tensed and through clenched teeth I said, "No! No shame on me! I told you not to say that to me!" Even though she apologized, I was furious and ready to end our relationship. I called Ed to vent my frustration. He listened and gave me godly counsel. I eventually calmed down.

The next day Ed came over to pray. "I had a vision last night," he said. "I saw a piece of flesh that had a *z*-shaped wound. Then I saw the word *PAIN*. The capital letters were white with jagged edges and they were centered over the wound. I was pulled back to get a birds-eye view. I realized the flesh was a human heart, and it had many scars from being repeatedly stabbed. That heart is yours.

"Part of the *z*-shaped wound is healing, as a scab has formed. Yet while it's still tender, the devil pierced it. The fresh stab wound caused your heart to react; it recoiled to protect itself from your mom's sharp words cutting into it again. Your reaction was not just righteous indignation. You reacted to pain and shock."

I lamented, "She broke her promise that she would never say those words again. I had hoped to be done with shame. I had hoped to be safe."

"The devil attacked you through your mom's words. She's always been his mouth-piece, speaking guilt and shame into your life. You need to realize those words are actually Satan's and not your mom's, and therefore they'll likely keep coming. You'll have to wedge the armor of God between yourself and your mom. It'll have to stay there until she changes or dies."

Ed began having serious health problems. He had become such a source of help and encouragement to me that I could hardly bare the fact that he seemed to be getting worse. I felt anxious, though I tried to keep my mind off his failing health. One night I woke at 4:30 a.m. filled with fear and panic that Ed might die. I got out of bed and prayed. Two hours later I finally fell back asleep. I didn't know why I reacted so strongly, since Ed had been having health problems off and on for some time. What I did know was that this anxiety had the enemy's signature all over it.

Soon after, Ed and I were able to get together and spend some time in prayer. I admitted to Ed that I was nearly debilitated by my fear of him dying, and I didn't want my life to fall apart if something happened to him. I longed for peace in this and all of life's tribulations. "How can I be filled with God's peace in the midst of trials?" I asked.

"In my spirit I saw your question go straight up to Heaven and into the throne room. I feel overwhelmed by the beauty of how God received it that I have to fight back tears."

As we prayed, God's revelation came through Ed. "The anxiety you had was another knee-jerk reaction, a behavior created by Satan. Satan taught you an unspoken language, a communication skill—fear and anxiety. He programmed you through your dad's words. When your dad worked the factory's assembly line, he inserted fear in your heart and as a result, fear became the foundation of your life."

Ed went on, "The past two years God has given you knowledge and has trained you. He's built a beautiful house for you to live in. Unfortunately, the house is built in a swamp—constructed on a foundation of fear. To live safely in your new house, the foundation needs to change."

Ed pulled a small bottle of anointing oil out of his pocket. "The purpose of this is symbolic, as a means of dredging out the swamp."

He rubbed oil on my forehead and prayed, "Thank you Lord for removing the foundation of fear and replacing it with your foundation of peace. Everything has been built on that fear foundation and it has to change. In the name of Jesus Christ, the Savior, the Deliverer, I break those curses, those words that embedded fear into the building blocks of Denise's life. I declare those foul words, those fearful words, are broken. I thank you God that you can replace fear with peace."

As he put the bottle back in his pocket, he said, "In my spirit I see words of fear stacked one on top of each other like pancakes. As a child, you were forced to eat each one of them, and as you consumed the fear, you learned that's what life is. That's just another lie. And you don't have to continue ingesting the fear. Just as you chose life or death, blessing or cursing, you can choose whether or not to swallow the devil's lies."

I decided I wouldn't let my past choose for me. I refused to allow my upbringing to have the final authority. Though fear had

I refused to allow my upbringing to have the final authority.

been a building block of my life and had become a knee-jerk reaction, I could still learn the language of peace.

We asked God how to remove my reflexive reaction to fear. God answered with, *Love covers a multitude.* We didn't understand how these were linked, so we continued to pray.

Suddenly Ed said, "It's wrong. It's wrong. I don't know what's wrong, but all I can say is wrong, wrong, wrong. Something is wrong. The wrong is unrighteous and it came from Satan. It shouldn't be there; it was inserted, instilled, infused into you."

After a moment of silence, Ed continued, "There are two parts to your foundation; one is fear, the other unworthiness. As a child and young adult, you concluded you were unworthy of love. You thought something was wrong with you or you weren't good enough, that's why you hated yourself and lived such a destructive life. Do you know that you're actually worthy of God's love? Little ole ugly, fearful, unwanted, it's-all-your-fault you."

I thought I had accepted that I was worthy of God's love.

"Are you worthy of God's peace?" Ed inquired.

"I think so, why wouldn't I be?" I replied.

"Your response is not emphatic enough. God's peace is your desire, not a state you're in. The problem is a decision you made as a child. I don't know the exact decision, but I know that you're worthy of God's love and peace, despite what you may have thought or decided. Jesus granted you His love and peace. You can accept it or refuse it."

God had given me His peace, but I unknowingly refused it because I still believed in the doctrines of fear and unworthiness. The knee-jerk reactions continued because my life was based on that prior conditioning. I didn't know how to get rid of the old foundation, but I knew I had the ability. My daughter was proof that I could change. I resisted that old familiar foundation as I parented Hannah, but I had not completely shaken it on a personal level. Tears started to roll down my cheeks. "I can't handle weeks or months of anxiety again," I sobbed.

When I quieted down, Ed prayed for me. "Lord, I pray that the enemy's lies will be exposed, that Denise will rescind her childhood decision, and that she'll accept your truths. Amen."

Ed challenged me to describe what was wrong with the way my dad treated me, and I was to watch how I felt in my heart. I told him that my dad treated me with contempt and hatred. He criticized me, tore me down, and made me feel bad about myself. It was wrong that he didn't love me. It was wrong that he didn't care about me. It was disgusting that he treated me worse than a dog.

Ed said, "Keep going, there's something you need to discover."

I continued, "The way he treated my mom was wrong. It was wrong that he wouldn't love me and that I couldn't touch him. It was wrong that he gave me a bad image of men. It was wrong that he instilled a distorted image of God in me. It was wrong that I didn't learn how to properly love because of him. It was wrong that he hurt my heart all the time and made me feel like worthless garbage."

Ed told me to talk a little bit more about my mom. When I spoke about her, he heard me gasp, as if I'd had an automatic reaction of some kind.

The truth is that I didn't like the way he treated my mom. He put fear and worry into her. Because of him, she felt bad about herself and unworthy of love—the same things I felt. He made her miserable and basically ruined her life. He damaged her so much so that she couldn't be a good mom to me.

Tears pooled in my eyes.

"And that hurts you because . . ." Ed prompted.

"It hurts because I love her, and I can't have a normal relationship with her because she's messed up. And he hasn't changed; he still degrades her and criticizes her. I want him to stop hurting her. I want him to stop making her miserable. When I was young we waited for him to die, so we could have normal lives and be happy. But he just kept living. We thought because he was so much older than my mom, he would die soon, and then we could enjoy our lives."

My tears turned into sobs. I sank to the floor and buried my face in my hands.

"Oh, those words," Ed exclaimed. "The power in that last sentence overwhelms me." He stumbled around the room breathing deeply. Through his breathlessness he stammered, "The decision, I saw the decision!"

I knew what Ed was talking about. I saw it too. I had decided that I couldn't be happy until my dad died. I made that decision during my childhood and I didn't even remember it—until God pulled it out of me. My dad hadn't had authority in my life for over twenty-five years, but my decision was still in effect. It authorized him to have dominion over my joy and peace as long as he lived. With this revelation, I knew I needed to consciously rescind that decision. I could be happy and have peace whether my dad was dead or alive.

Our prayer room was thick with God's peace, so Ed joined me on the floor and we just sat for a while. After God's presence lifted, I told Ed, "I can tell that something has died inside me because my whole body is relaxed. Even so, I want to profess a decision to be happy and have peace."

I stood up and proclaimed, "By God's authority, I declare that I can be happy and that peace is mine. I choose to live in peace, and I see and hear peace all around me. My thoughts are peaceful and full of God's love. I love God my Father. He gives me peace, strength, and courage. He cleanses my soul. He leads me in paths of righteousness for His namesake and I follow Him. God is the only one who has authority over me and I yield myself to Him."

God is the only one who has authority over me and I yield myself to Him.

As a means of cleansing my heart, I needed to declare some things to my dad. I said, "Dad, I refuse your lies. They have no value to me, no hold on me, and no authority over me. I refuse to listen or react to your lies anymore, and I will never fall for them again. I am free from you and the fear you created!"

As we circled around, God imparted knowledge into Ed. "There's still an authority structure in place. In my spirit I see an organizational chart. Your dad is at the top, your mom is below him, and the kids are at the bottom. You have to take yourself out of that chain of command."

I quickly blurted out, "Dad, I quit! I am no longer your submissive daughter, so you have no authority in my life."

Ed responded, "Authority is the right to command someone— and your dad has no right to command you. His commands were not only spoken orders, but they were trigger words and phrases, his body language, and his presence. If he tries to exercise his once powerful authority, his commands will now carry no weight.

"Have you realized that though you're his child, you're helping to care for him as he gets older, and therefore you have some authority over him?"

Ed was right. At times my dad asked me for help with medical problems, medications, and taking him to appointments. He didn't respect me, yet he seemed to respect my sister. I thought it was due to money. She's wealthy, and I'm not.

Ed corrected me. "The real reason is because she stands up to his authority and you submit to it."

I told Ed about a recent incident where I stood up to my dad. He said something inappropriate in front of Hannah, and I told him she didn't need to learn that at her age. He retorted that she may as well learn it now since she'll learn it sooner or later. I told him that I decided when she learned things, not him. He didn't listen and continued to argue with me. I told him we were going to leave, and then my mom intervened.

Ed said, "He didn't respect you when you opposed him because you were like an employee standing up to your boss. Now you're no longer in his organizational chart and submissive to him. You won't be standing up to him like he's your boss anymore. You'll be talking to your subordinate.

"Let's go back to the organization chart. I'm convinced you're no longer in your dad's chart. Not only is the line from him to you erased, but your name is completely gone. And there's a new chart. On this reorganized chart, God the Father, God the Son, and God the Holy Spirit are at the top. They all connect down to you as you're directly under them. Hannah's next to you, though slightly below you, and your other family members, including your parents, are underneath the two of you. This is a righteous chart. It's God's chart, and He is the authority over you. His peace, love, joy, and all the fruit of the Spirit connect directly to you, so when trials and tribulations come, you now take them to your new Boss.

"But wait. There's a dotted line connecting you to the old chart. The dotted line is love. This love has to be managed. Your love can flow to them, but you have to refuse everything that comes from the old chart. Your heart has to have a door of protection on it—your safety has to be above your need for their love. This is critical."

I realized I had been robbed of a lifetime of peace and happiness, and my heart grieved. Yet the next few days, God's love permeated me. I felt free, like a slave released from a tyrant.

The one remaining piece of anxiety I had was about Ed's health. Had I decided I would only be safe and secure if Ed was alive? Did I trust Ed more than God? I wanted the fear of his death out of my heart, because even if he didn't die soon, he would die someday. I needed peace in the midst of my friend's failing health.

During our next prayer session, I told Ed about this. He said, "I see a picture of your brother in my mind. Tell me about him."

My half-brother Dan unexpectedly left home when I was eight. I remembered my mom told me he went to live with his dad, and I ran to my room and bawled. I loved my brother. My heart broke when he left.

God's wisdom came through Ed. "Dan wasn't like the rest of your family; he loved you unconditionally. He kept your heart alive in the midst of neglect, shame, and rejection. He was a light in your dark world, he provided safe love—and then he was gone. You didn't anticipate being abandoned. Your safe harbor silently deserted you."

I chimed in, "And now you've become my shelter. When my crisis hit I turned to you for help, and you proved yourself safe and dependable. In the hardest time of my life you prayed with me, encouraged and supported me, and responded every time I called. You have never let me down."

Ed looked slightly embarrassed, but I continued anyway. "It's been just over two years since I first called you to help me fight the devil. You're my security blanket. I know if things ever get bad again, I can count on you."

Ed interjected, "You think that if I die your life will fall apart—like it did when your brother left. You'll be alone and have no one to help you. The truth is I haven't helped you; the Holy Spirit has worked through me to bring you to this place of restoration. You have the same Holy Spirit in you.

"Since Dan and I have similar characteristics, you've transposed the experience and anguish you had with him onto me. Like a movie you've already seen, you know the ending, and it left you devastated. Expecting your life to crumble when I die is powerful and it carries authority. It's like a self-fulfilling prophecy—but it's flawed.

"To continue with the movie analogy, Dan's movie ended abruptly and you were left alone with no love or security. You expect my movie to end the same way, except it can't; we have a righteous author writing our story. Our movie cast list includes the Father, Son, and Holy Spirit. All that to say you won't be alone when I die. You have a loving Father who watches over you with great care and He will never leave you. What's more, you have your Friend Jesus, and the Holy Spirit your Comforter."

I took a deep sigh and smiled. "God is so amazing. As you told this simple yet powerful analogy, I felt the fear of you dying get pushed out of my heart. But I still have to recover from the pain Dan caused when he left. My brother suffered physical and verbal abuse by my dad so I don't fault him for leaving. He was likely motivated by self-preservation and just packed up his stuff and left. I understand that he didn't have time to worry about his little sister, but I still felt deserted by him."

Ed replied, "I sense God is doing intimate open-heart surgery in you. I have a vision of your heart again. One of the stab wounds is being operated on today. Let me ask you this, what kind of nightmare would have played out if your brother had stayed and retaliated against your dad and killed him?"

His question surprised me, but I thought through the possibilities. Dan would have gone to prison. My mom most likely would have had a nervous breakdown. We would have lost our home. Dawn and I may have been placed in foster care. My school may have changed. I'd be emotionally scarred, especially if I witnessed the bloodshed. My life would have been a complete disaster.

With this new perspective, I no longer felt devastated that Dan left. His departure was actually an act of love because he knew what he was capable of doing. My brother's movie ended the best it could. It was the best God could do with people who didn't know Him.

I was in awe of God's faithfulness and goodness to me—even then. My heart felt happy. The Light had come in, causing the devil's oppression to depart. And my wound was healed. Only God could have turned that lie into freedom.

As we walked upstairs, Ed said, "You're a good Christian mom, Denise."

"Thanks," I replied.

"Why won't you receive that?"

"I did," I snapped.

"In my spirit I saw you rebuff it. And I perceive you're feeling defensive."

I didn't agree with Ed, but I knew well enough to know that God was speaking to him.

Ed explained, "Your defensiveness is yet another knee-jerk reaction. This one is directed at the value of *good*. *Good* does nothing more than describe you, but it doesn't line up with the picture your parents and others painted of you, the picture you still have of yourself. It's like looking at a negative from a film camera; the colors are inaccurate and the details are blurry, making it difficult to distinguish the actual picture."

As God's truth penetrated my heart, I conceded. I understood why I rejected Ed's comment and why I hated compliments. To receive an accolade I would have to agree with it, and disagree with a building block of my life.

My self-image was shaped when I was young, but it started to change when I met Jesus. To completely develop my picture I had to take the negatives (the wrong things I believed about myself) and expose them to the Light and wash them in the blood of Christ. Then my self-portrait would be accurate; the colors bright, the details sharp, the true

To completely develop my picture I had to take the negatives (the wrong things I believed about myself) and expose them to the Light.

beauty revealed. If I kept my negative self-image, I would be saying God's miraculous work hadn't changed me. I would not ignore what God had done.

Ed said, "There's some self-condemnation because you've learned to speak the family language about yourself. Your family placed little value on you and you not only accepted it, you agreed with it. The words they spoke and the tears you shed can't be changed, but you can reject their value judgment about you. That entails seeing yourself through God's eyes and accepting the high value He places on you. You also condemn yourself because you think you're like your parents. Satan planned for you to be like your parents and he squeezed you into a mold that looks like them. But you were never like them—that's why you rebelled against them when you got older."

Ed continued, "I see a vision of you. You're lying face down in a swamp. Muck coats the back of your head because you've been living below the surface. You lift your head up and see a field. The grass and trees look beautiful. Then you look down and see where you are. You realize you would rather live in the field under a big oak tree. You find the courage and strength to stand up and walk toward the land. The muck is deep and you have a ways to walk yet, but your desire will get you there.

"The enemy's plan to smother the real you in a swamp of fear will not prevail. God is taking the house He's built, you, out of the swamp because it doesn't belong there. You belong on a peaceful foundation under the big oak tree with Him. The grassy knoll will be your new home."

Life had settled down again—until one day, when I was walking from my car to my work place. I encountered resistance, a spiritual force pushing against me to keep me from entering the building. The closer I got, the more I noticed it. I didn't know why it was there, but I had no option other than to push on. I had to go to work.

As I walked into the clinic area, I heard God's soft voice speak to my spirit. *What are you doing here? You should be at home writing a book.*

What! God wanted me to quit my job and write a book?!

That was no small mandate. As a single mom with mortgage payments and my daughter in private school, I hesitated. But I trusted God; He had been faithful to me.

I consulted with Ed. He suggested I take a leave of absence instead. I knew in my spirit that was wrong, so I gave my resignation. Then fear rushed in. Did I not trust God as much as I thought? I asked Ed to pray with me.

Ed said, "In my spirit I see you in a defensive stance. Your hands are in front of your face to protect you from something, or some-one—God."

Why would I defend myself against God, I wondered?

Ed brought up his experience in Vietnam. "I wasn't a Christian then, and I was furious with God. I actually hated Him because of what happened there. Surrounded by the devil's work, I blamed God for the evil I saw. I mistakenly thought that God could do whatever He wanted and was therefore responsible for those atrocities."

As Ed talked I got choked up inside. I knew he was on the right track. God revealed that I'd had a similar misconception. As a child, I learned that God was all-knowing and all-powerful. At the same time, my dad ruled over me, and I was subject to his abuse. I assumed my childhood must have been God's plan because He knew about it and had the power to change my situation, if He wanted. I concluded that since He chose not to, that He was responsible for what happened.

Ed continued, "You concluded that bad things come through those in authority. This belief that authority might cause you harm is still hidden in your heart. You're reluctant to quit your job, and you put your hands up to protect yourself from God, your authority, because you learned to trust bad things would happen—even with obedience."

I refuted this because I trusted God for good things. I had obeyed Him many times, including adopting my daughter from China, and nothing bad happened. But as we examined my trip to China, I saw that I really hadn't trusted God. I was terrified by the seventeen hour flight. As I boarded the plane, I told myself that if I didn't go, I could never talk to God again. I decided I would rather get on the plane and die then live without God.

Ed said, "You obeyed God out of fear of repercussions, just as you'd done with your dad. Don't feel bad, you weren't really obeying Him out of fear, you were conditioned. Your childhood church taught you not to sin for fear of God's wrath, and you obeyed your dad out of fear, not because you loved him. They both coerced you into obedience by instilling a fear of negative consequences. God wants you to obey Him out of love and know that obedience to Him is for your benefit."

I felt relieved knowing there would be no repercussions—no matter what I did with my job. However, I knew that God would continue to lead me in the direction He desired me to go. I told Ed, "I want to trust God enough to do whatever He tells me to do, but something's holding me back."

Ed replied, "As a follower of Jesus, you're not supposed to trust in your job or in money, you're to trust God for your provision. I don't think you've ever really trusted God as your provider. As a child, you slept in your dad's house and ate his food, but you couldn't trust him. Now you're unable to trust God to provide for you because you couldn't trust your dad when he was your provider. But God has already been providing for you. During your childhood, He kept you safe and gave you a brother who loved you. As you got older, He kept you alive when you put yourself in dangerous situations. He provided for you when you didn't know Him or trust Him, and He's still providing for you. He can't help Himself, that's who He is—your Provider" (Phil. 4:19).

I realized that if I could completely trust God, I'd have no fear or worry about anything, and the devil couldn't touch me. I wanted that true peace in the midst of life's trials. I decided not to withdraw my resignation. I was stepping out of the boat and walking toward my Provider.

One morning at church, the pastor's sermon focused on fear being linked to control. He asked us to look at what we tried to control, and told us if we released our grip on those parts of our lives, God would deliver us from fear in those areas. I realized that though I had submitted myself to God, I still tried to control many things in my life. I needed to surrender not just my-

I realized that if I could completely trust God, I'd have no fear or worry about anything, and the devil couldn't touch me.

self and my job, but *all* I held in my hand. That would be complete trust in God and banish any leftover fear.

When I checked my e-mail later, I had a message from Ed. God had given him a word of knowledge about me:

"You weren't able to control your relationship with your dad and you got hurt. Since then, you've had to be in charge in your relationships, otherwise you don't feel safe.

God initiated your relationship with Him when Jesus stood at the door of your heart and knocked. You chose to let Him into your heart and life. Like most Christians you control your relationship with God, but He never intended you to. God is supposed to control your relationship, and you are to submit to and follow Him— in the intimate and powerful times, and in the quiet seasons."

Two different people had given me the same message. Clearly, God intended for me to hear this! He wanted me to give up control of the things in my life to Him—then I would be completely surrendered. But complete surrender required complete trust. Could I not completely trust God after all He had done for me? If God hadn't intervened during my crisis, I'd likely be dead. I literally owed God my life. As His grateful daughter, I would give it all to Him.

During my prayer time, I turned my ottoman into an altar. I laid out my stethoscope to symbolize my career, my wallet to symbolize my finances, a Lincoln Log roof to symbolize my home, and a book to symbolize my obedience to writing this book. I also set on it pictures of my parents and Hannah as well as dolls to represent myself, my brother and sister, and Ed.

Complete surrender required complete trust.

I knelt before my make-shift altar and raised my hands. "Father, I relinquish control of my career and money, my house and all the possessions in it, the writing of the book, and my loved ones lives; their health, behaviors, and salvation. I let go of them and entrust them to you."

I sat quietly before the altar. I felt God reassuring me that I was His child and it was His responsibility to take care of me just as I took care of Hannah. Unfortunately, He couldn't fully do that if I didn't let Him. As His child, I was to be a vessel for His glory, but I couldn't carry His glory if I held onto those other things. They were like anchors weighing me down.

An hour later a nurse called me from a local emergency room. Ed had been visiting a sick friend at the hospital and the ceiling collapsed on him causing head and neck injuries. I stayed calm and prayed for him. On my drive to the hospital, I realized I wasn't afraid of Ed dying. My heart was at peace.

Ed suffered a concussion and spent a few days in the hospital. With my life on the altar, I wasn't worried about what might happen to me if Ed died, so I was free to genuinely care about him. When he felt better, I shared with him my experience at the make-shift altar. God gave him a word of knowledge: "You've cast your crowns," he said.

By taking my crowns off and laying them at the feet of Jesus, I had stepped down as king and gave Him control over what those crowns represented. When it came to my last day on the job, I had no fear. I felt light and peaceful inside.

It took Ed months to fully recover from his injuries, but during that time, he sent me a very poignant e-mail:

"Satan molded your character—he changed you from who you were supposed to be. But each battle you have gone through has moved you toward God's original design. With each step you walked away from the old you that Satan used to rule over, to the new you strolling shoulder to shoulder with the Son of God.

Unfortunately, your perspective of you is still based on your childhood. There is something hidden yet that keeps you seeing yourself in a distorted way. You still see yourself as unworthy, but you are special and important to God."

I was taken aback by the message that I was special and important to God. Throughout my life no one had ever told me that I was important, and I had never thought of myself that way. Initially I thought I was important to God because I was useful to Him, but then realized I was important to God because He loved me.

A few days later Ed came over to pray. I agreed with him that my perspective had more room for improvement. My sense of self-worth still fluctuated with my circumstances. I told him that I wanted my self-worth to be fully developed.

Ed replied, "That word *developed* exploded in my spirit. You're not changing as your self-worth develops; you're being restored back to the garden—returning to the person God created you as."

Ed went on, "I see an image of a black box. The box is an assault perpetrated on your life. The box was formed as your dad mistreated you, and it contains the negative picture he painted of you. You believed that's who you are and it became part of you. Your dad was used by Satan to put this box on your path as a stumbling block."

It was discouraging to me that the stumbling block was still there after two and a half years of God replacing lies with truth.

I thought I was important to God because I was useful to Him, but then realized I was important to God because He loved me.

Ed continued, "It's preventing you from believing you're important to God and therefore becoming who God created you to be. The box is a lie, designed to trip you up as you skip down your steppingstones toward God and His will for your life.

"I suddenly feel very sad. I sense the devil continually whispers to you, *Look at the box, keep your eye on the box.* Now I see an image of a white box. It contains the picture God painted of you—as He created you. You're headed toward the white box, but the black box with your stained picture of you is in the way. To get beyond the black box, forgiveness is needed. You've already forgiven your dad for what he's done to you, but you need to forgive him for who he made you into. This will allow you to let go of your erroneous picture and walk past the black box to God's white box."

I confessed out loud, "Dad, I forgive you for tainting my picture and making me see myself as unworthy and unimportant. I forgive you for forming that black box, but I am not the person you said I was, and I refuse to keep your picture of me. Father God, I will follow your picture of me because your picture of me is accurate. Help me to see myself as you see me and continue to change me so I look like the person you created me to be."

Ed wanted me to visualize the time I was peering down the hallway to watch my dad shave and he shut the bathroom door on me. Ed asked, "Can you tell your dad that wasn't important to you?"

I thrust my arms out as if to push a door open and said, "You're not slamming that door in my face! I will not let you shut the door on me because I am walking away from you and your lies today."

Ed was convinced that this declaration altered the course of my life as much as any of the other changes I had made. It was true. With this final blow, God broke the chain that held the suffering girl captive in my heart. She was finally free.

New Territory

*Who knows whether you have come to the kingdom
for such a time as this?*
—Esther 4:14

THE NEXT SIX MONTHS, Ed and I only prayed together a handful of times. I told him I felt I didn't want to pray with him as often, but I wasn't sure why. In Ed's private prayer time, God assured him I was ready to get out from behind his shadow. There was a time when I needed to follow Ed, but we were on equal ground now, so God required a change from our old method of prayer. What a relief. Now I knew why I didn't want to pray with Ed. It also confirmed that what I was feeling was actually God leading me into new territory.

I also felt like I wanted to build on the foundation of knowledge that God had laid. I was grateful God rescued and restored me, but I didn't want it to stop there. I wanted my life in Christ to go deeper. This was a God-given desire. To go along with my strong prayer life and changing character, God was going to teach me to listen to my spirit and to be obedient to Him.

I went to visit a friend who was somewhat familiar with my recent experiences. I told her some more details. We talked for six hours, but it could have been six days. She had a lot of questions about salvation, authority, deception, past hurts, and relationships. I didn't have all the answers, but I knew God spoke many things to her through me.

Shortly before I left, my friend said, "You look so pretty today, Denise. Have you done something different with your hair?"

I dismissed her comment, "Honestly, I look terrible today; I'm not wearing make-up and my hair is scraggly because I got caught in the rain earlier."

She persisted, "Even your teeth look different from earlier today. It's as if you're getting prettier as the day goes on."

I think the longer I talked about what God had done for me, the more He shined through me. I was radiant because of Christ in me, and He was the one who looked attractive to her!

One day I was visiting with a former colleague. Our conversation became rather personal when she told me she was contemplating whether she should get a new job or go back school. She said she wasn't horribly unhappy, but something was definitely missing in her life. She'd been trying to find fulfillment with her boyfriend and career, but wasn't satisfied with either. She even wondered if getting a dog would help fill the void.

As she talked, I knew in my spirit that God wanted me to tell her about Him. When she finished speaking, I told her I had gone

through the same thing. I had looked for satisfaction in men, in edu-
cation, in my job, and in material possessions. I explained that these
were futile ambitions, and I was empty until I met God. I explained
the God-shaped hole we have inside us, and told her she couldn't be
content until it was filled with God. I testified to who I was before
Christ and how God had changed me. I knew by the look on her
face that what I said rang true to her. I could also tell that she didn't
expect to hear that God was her answer.

When she left, I was speechless. I had talked to many people
about God before, but this was different. This conversation was spirit-
led and felt natural and relaxed, not forced by me or anyone else. I
wasn't outwardly ecstatic, just so incredibly thankful and honored that
God had used me. He was taking what had been a broken, worthless
life and was turning it into something beautiful. I wept.

A few days later Hannah and I were walking toward the grocery store.
A school bus was parked in front of the store, and I wondered why it
was there. I strained to see who might be inside. I saw a child sitting
by the window, leaning his head on a large head rest. He had a dis-
ability of some kind. I saw another child whose neck and face were
twisted. They were endearing to me until I was struck with this overwhelmingly strong sense of evil and was forced to look away. I felt
grieved at the same time.

My spirit clearly discerned something, and I felt the urge to pray
for those children. My mind was full of excuses. I couldn't go on the
bus. Hannah was with me. I did not listen to the nudging of the Holy
Spirit that day. I did nothing.

I realized the significance of this later. God had given me an opportunity to do what had been done for me—to pray for and deliver someone oppressed by the devil. The sadness I had experienced was God's heart for the children. To say I regretted not praying for them would be an understatement, but there was no condemnation. I was learning. Next time I would follow through.

Hannah and I often went swimming at our local community center pool. On one particular occasion, as we splashed around, I noticed a girl approximately three years old, who had an obvious medical condition. I didn't know what afflicted her, but her body was constantly moving and she was unable to support herself in the water without help. I became mesmerized by this little girl. As I stared at her, I felt four or five sharp jabs of intense grief, as if someone had grabbed my heart and squeezed it tightly. I fought hard to control my emotions. After the waves of agony passed, I fixed my gaze on her again. I sympathized with her pain and hardship. In my mind I heard, *Why don't you do something about this?*

I didn't know if God was speaking to me or if that was my own thought, but I contemplated what to do. I could ask her mom if I could pray for her. If I did that, I would have to take Hannah with me or have her sit on the side of the pool and wait. As I considered my options, they headed out of the water. I realized the woman with the child was a therapist when she took her to her mother who was sitting poolside. As they left, I remembered I didn't have to lay hands on her or pray a long fancy prayer, so I simply said, "God, heal this child, in the name of Jesus."

Later in the day I evaluated what happened. I couldn't make sense of the grief I had felt, but I concluded that question was from God and I should have done something. I called Ed and asked him to pray with me about this.

When Ed arrived, I told him the details of what happened at the pool and after a moment of silence he said, "We need to understand the question, 'Why don't you do something about this?'"

Revelation came through Ed as we prayed, "That question is not about the girl; it's about you. God didn't ask the question to prompt you to do something; it was to help you understand *why* you didn't do anything. Were you afraid, or did you think it wasn't your place to intervene, or did you lack the assertiveness needed to pray for her?"

I contemplated Ed's questions and said, "I didn't consider what others might have thought nor did I doubt my ability to pray for her. The reason I didn't do anything was because I was mesmerized by the girl and had difficulty comprehending what was happening."

Ed said, "You weren't mesmerized by the girl or her condition. You were mesmerized because you sensed the overwhelming power of God's compassion. Although you tried to analyze this power, it was beyond your logic and reason. Additionally, the intense grief you fought so hard to keep inside was God's anguish over the girl."

Ed continued, "I hear *capacity* in my spirit. And I see a glass beaker in my mind. God is pouring His compassion into the beaker, until it's so full that one more drop would make it spill over. Now God is pouring in more, and it's overflowing. That's a picture of you. God filled you to capacity with His compassion, and when He poured in more, the excess spilled out as waves of intense grief."

I remembered the Bible says in many places that Jesus healed people because He had compassion on them. Jesus couldn't help Himself. Filled with God's compassion, He was moved to heal. God's compassion didn't give Jesus the power to heal, it gave Him the impetus. I wondered if that was why God filled me with His compassion, so I would do something and He could heal the girl.

Ed said, "Let's examine both the boy on the bus and the girl in the pool for similarities."

As we talked about each scenario, it became apparent that the rest of the environment had faded away, time seemed to have slowed down, and I focused only on the children. I didn't see them with my natural eyes, but with the eyes of my spirit, and my spirit locked onto them. I didn't know anything spiritual was happening when these events occurred which is why I didn't do anything about them. I wasn't experienced enough, and I didn't understand what God wanted.

God had told me multiple times to more fully walk in the spirit. This served as another reminder for me.

Hannah and I were back at the pool the following week. This time Hannah had her swim lesson, and I leisurely swam around. The girl I'd seen the week before was with her therapist again. I watched her, but I wasn't mesmerized, and there was no intense grief or compassion. The young girl was beautiful, with curly blond hair and big blue eyes. She had skinny arms and legs that shook nonstop.

I was surprised when our eyes locked. Someone or something inside her looked at me. There was an unspoken communication between us. It knew me, and I recognized it. When her therapist brought her close to where I was swimming, my spirit became repulsed by the evil I sensed.

Last week I experienced God's broken heart for this girl and His compassion spilled out of me. This week I perceived the enemy in her. Next week I would come prepared.

I formulated a plan. While Hannah was in her lesson and the girl had her therapy, I would talk with her mother and ask if I could pray for her daughter. If the mom agreed, I would pray for her child when she finished her therapy. Every night I thought about that little girl and my heart ached. I imagined how the scenario might play out, and what great joy there would be if she was healed.

Finally the big day came. I got Hannah settled in her lesson, and as I sat down I saw the girl's mother sitting on the other side of the pool. I started to ask God what He wanted me to do, but before I finished my sentence, I began walking toward her. As I took a seat near her, her cell phone rang. While I waited, I watched her daughter's therapy session. I resolved that evil thing was going to come out of her.

Her mother and I had a great conversation; she was friendly and had a kind heart. Her daughter's name was Sophie and she had Rett Syndrome, a genetic neurodevelopmental disorder that primarily affects girls. When she said her daughter's condition was hereditary, I thought, *If it's genetic, then it can't be a demon.* She went on to tell me how it was diagnosed, what her symptoms were, and how doctors were treating it. Her eyes glistened with tears when she told me Sophie had a life expectancy of twenty.

Our time was running out, so I asked her if I could pray for Sophie. She said yes. When the therapist brought Sophie back to her mom, I felt repulsed by the evil I sensed, and I didn't want to touch her. But after she was wrapped in a towel, I put my hand on her head and prayed that God's love and compassion would flow into her and heal her. When I finished, her mother thanked me and we parted.

I had no joy or excitement. I had accomplished my goal of praying for the child, but something was left undone. I reviewed what happened. I had obeyed God and prayed for the girl. I wasn't embarrassed or self-conscious when I prayed, and when I left I didn't look around to see if anyone had been watching. I didn't even consider what others thought of me or what I was doing. That was a huge change for me!

But I had made a big mistake. My thought, *If it's genetic, then it can't be a demon* wasn't really mine. Satan had whispered a lie in my ear and it shut down my intent to cast a demon out of her. Instead of exercising God's authority, I prayed a sweet, passive prayer. Also, I felt God's anointing leave while I was praying for her and something in my spirit shriveled up. I'm afraid I grieved the Holy Spirit. Next time I would do it right.

For two weeks I looked for Sophie. She was never there. I had asked God to forgive me for my mistake and I knew He did, but I blamed myself that the girl was still in that tormented condition. I grieved over her. Ed knew what had happened, and he thought we should pray.

Like so many times before, God imparted His wisdom to Ed. "You see your faults more readily than you see the good things you do. In your eyes, the good things you've done can be held in a teacup, while you pile up your failures by the basketful. Your accomplishments carry little weight because your dad forced a paradigm of performance on you, and you're hanging on to remnants of that mindset. Though you see your baskets of failures outweighing your teacup of accomplishments, God doesn't see you that way. God wants you to know that you didn't fail with Sophie. You didn't do everything right, but you stepped out and grew in the process. You're to see this experience as a lesson, and apply what you've learned in the future."

Ed stopped walking and stared at the floor. Then he looked up at me and asked, "Do you see yourself dressed in the robe of righteousness God gave you?"

The truth was it varied. Since I'd messed up with Sophie, I didn't see myself in the robe of righteousness, but when things went well I did.

Ed said, "Remember, your righteousness is not based on how you feel and it doesn't waver with success and failure. Because you carry your failures in your heart, you've wrapped it in rags of failure, rags of unrighteousness. Your heart is cloaked in rags. You can't wear them anymore."

Your righteousness is not based on how you feel and it doesn't waver with success and failure.

"I don't want to. How can I get rid of them?"

Ed asked, "How did you decide to divorce your husband?"

"I told my husband I would leave him if he got charged with another DUI. My decision was firm in my heart, so the next time he got arrested, the decision was already made. I left."

"With your ex-husband your decision was final and you never looked back, but you often change your mind about your righteousness based on your performance. You need to divorce these rags of failure like you did your husband; admit they're detrimental to your life, and decide the lie of performance-based righteousness has to go—permanently. You need to refuse and rebuke the curse of performance-based righteousness."

I was ready to get rid of the rags!

"You can't do this with your mind," Ed warned. "Your heart has to speak to the rags that cover it."

As Ed stood to one side of the room, I prayed in tongues and walked our circled path. I envisioned rags hanging off my heart, like a zombie covered in tatters of death. Then I said, "In the name of Jesus, I rebuke you Satan. Take those rags off my heart. I refuse to wear those rags anymore."

Ed admonished me. "Don't tell Satan to take them off, *you* rip them off."

I said, "You stink. You're foul. You're disgusting. I rip you off my heart and tear you to shreds. I pound and stomp on you and throw you into the fire—right into Hell! Get off my heart and stay off!"

The rags came off because I got mad and exercised my authority. I knew I had spoken from my heart because my mind was surprised by what my mouth said.

Almost three years had passed since the night of the crisis. God recently prompted me to consider a degree in ministry. I took His direction seriously and began classes at a local Christian college. During my coursework, I was required to do an internship. I felt led to train with a chaplain to pray for sick people.

As I looked at various healthcare settings in which I might intern with a chaplain, I got sidetracked and began looking at jobs for a nurse practitioner—a degree I already held. I didn't see many opportunities that fit my needs and skills and began to feel fearful that if or when I needed to return to my first profession, that I would not be able to find a job. The panic I felt didn't make sense; it came fast and was out of proportion to my situation. I didn't even need a job right then. Besides, God led me down this jobless road, and I trusted He would walk it with me. He would not let me become a homeless single mother.

God spoke to me through Ed in our next prayer session. "The panic you're experiencing is rooted in the fear of not surviving. But the panic you have isn't yours; it's a knee-jerk reaction triggered by a seed that was planted long ago. This seed is the fear of death, and it causes you to react with panic when you think your well-being is in danger. This programmed response is part of your old man."

As a child, my home was unsafe and so I learned not to trust anyone to take care of me. I decided to be in charge of my life. I put my safety and life in my own hands.

I remembered when I was fifteen and at my boyfriend's house. His mom was supposed to take me home at 10:00 p.m., but she called saying she had to work late. I knew my parents would be angry if I didn't make curfew, so my only option was to hitchhike home. I hoped he would offer to come with me. Instead he handed me a knife so I could protect myself and sent me away. I was on my own, with my safety in jeopardy again. Over the years this seed, this fear of death, was watered and reinforced many times.

Fear of death propagates in us when we're alienated from God. As a child of God, that fear should've vanished, but the enemy twisted it and worked it into a weapon. It affected my relationship with God. I trusted God enough to quit my job, but panic was able to grip my heart because my decision to depend on myself was still in effect, and it prevented me from fully relying on God. I was trusting God with everything *in* my life, but not *with* my life. Shouldn't I trust God with my life and my death?

I told Ed, "Since this panic started, I've been reminding myself of the things I put on my altar—I surrendered my whole life to God."

Ed replied, "You didn't put your death on the altar. You put yourself on there, but with you came the old decision of self-reliance. You have to dig up the seed by renouncing your fear of death—then the knee-jerk reaction to panic will cease to exist. You also have to nullify your previous decision by committing your death into God's hands. Your death, as everyone else's, will be God's responsibility, so you won't have to bear the burden of trying to stay alive. These actions will not only eradicate your fear of death, but other fears in life as well."

I knelt down, lifted my hands, and prayed, "Father, I submit my death into your hands. I put my death on the altar next to my life and all the other things I've entrusted to you. I can't be responsible for my death, so I ask you to help me let go of it. I proclaim I will no longer fear death or fret about surviving. I ask you to replace that fear with peace. I trust that my death will occur in your timing and your manner, and when my time comes I will fall into Jesus's arms."

Even with all my progress, I started hearing negative thoughts about God, Ed, and even my daughter. The devil was also saying things I couldn't decipher. Along with the voices, I'd been feeling tired all week. I didn't go to the gym, Hannah and I didn't go ice skating as we had planned, and I didn't have energy to do my homework. I started yawning so much that it was embarrassing.

I was more than fed up with hearing offensive words. I aggressively prayed against those demons. They left, but I sensed they had done some damage.

I spent the next day writing. The words came easily for me and I should have been ecstatic. I was still feeling so physically tired that

I couldn't even be thankful. Something was wrong. I was being oppressed. I asked Ed to come over and pray with me about this.

By the Spirit of God, Ed explained, "The incomprehensible words you perceived were the devil's subtle suggestions that you're tired. You couldn't refuse his words because they were indiscernible. And even though you couldn't understand them, they still affected you."

As simple as that sounded, I knew in my spirit it was true. After Ed left, I spent time doing my nightly praise and worship. I had so much energy that I put on a full concert for God. The oppression was gone—with just a word from God!

I was flabbergasted and had many questions. I wondered how the devil's suggestions could cause a physical reaction in my body. Was this how the devil caused sickness, by giving subtle suggestions until symptoms manifested? If the devil repeatedly told me I had a headache, would I get a headache? If he spoke cancer to my cells, would they mutate? Why couldn't I discern his words? Why did the oppression leave just because God told me what the devil had been saying? Could I have broken it off myself?

I didn't get answers to these questions, but God shed some light on my situation. I didn't suddenly get tired. The fatigue had been building from the devil's subtle yet steady stream of suggestions and the cumulative effect had finally manifested. When I felt fatigued, it didn't raise a red flag initially as it had believability. My schedule *was* tiring; I was home schooling Hannah, writing a book, and going to college—not to mention running our household all by myself. I rationalized that perhaps I was doing too much for someone my age, and I needed a break to reenergize.

When the devil whispered to me that I was tired, it affected how I felt, what I thought, what I did, and what I didn't do. If that had continued, my course would likely have been altered. I may not have finished this book or continued with school. I wondered how many Christian's drag themselves to the finish line because they are so very weary.

This might be one of Satan's best kept secrets. He subtly, yet steadily, steals people's lives by making suggestions that take them out of the race, or at least slow them down—and they don't even know it.

I had always wanted to know the secrets and mysteries of God, but I realized it was almost as important to learn the devil's secrets. How could I fend him off if I didn't know how he operated?

The fatigue was gone, and I was motivated to write. The writing didn't flow very well, but I was determined to continue. Over and over I made changes, changed it back, only to change it again. Other times I just stared at my computer screen because I didn't know what to write. The material seemed almost foreign. I realized that God's anointing had left me, but I didn't know why. I called Ed to talk about it.

Filled with God's wisdom, Ed replied, "God has paused the writing process for a reason, and it's important. I hear the word *prepare* in my spirit. To prepare means to make ready, to become equipped for something that hasn't happened yet. You must prepare with prayer—get ready for something you're not prepared for."

Ed continued, "A two-edged sword is powerful in the hands of a well-trained and experienced warrior, but it's cumbersome for a novice. Though you've been fighting the enemy for years, your sword-wielding skills still need to be enhanced as you're not prepared for this bigger battle yet to come."

The next day Ed called me. He frantically said, "I had a dream that you were in danger. It was so real I had to call to see if you're all right. I dreamt there was a calamitous event; it had the flavor of Armageddon. God has equipped you for it, but you're not prepared. You must prepare!

"I sense this coming event isn't devised by God and it's not His will. Nevertheless, God will prepare you to survive it. To accomplish what God wants you to do, you have to cross a barrier—a barrier you can't see. Crossing this invisible resistance is your task. Prayer is the vehicle to break down this barrier and it will take you from where you are to another place beyond the barrier—to where God wants you to be. Don't worry, Denise. God wouldn't tell you to do this if you weren't capable."

"If prayer is all that's needed to get past the barrier, why am I not past it by now?" I asked.

"Because you have to cut down the barrier with your sword and push your way through to the new place—take your warfare to a new level. You won't understand the spiritual implications of this, but it's imperative that you ignore your mind's resistance and be aggressive like you're fighting a battle. Aggressiveness is the mechanism to get beyond that barrier. Once you break through, you'll be beyond that limitation and have a new ability."

Ed added, "After that, you can develop proficiency in spiritual warfare. This proficiency will affect your life and ministry. It will enable you to quickly adapt to rapidly changing conditions or new situations, giving you the ability to avoid or get out of danger."

That night I prayed in tongues more aggressively than I ever had before. I prayed as if my life depended on it. I was angry and yelled like a mad woman. My blood pressure must have risen about fifty points! In all my battles with the devil, I had never prayed like this. I knew the barrier was destroyed!!

Previously, I had been writing three hours a day, but God had reassigned me to engage in spiritual warfare. With so much time to practice, I quickly became proficient and confident in my new place I called "the zone."

In this place I exercised my authority over the devil by speaking commands to him in tongues. Though I still fiercely wielded my sword, I didn't get worked up like I did when I destroyed the barrier. I didn't have to; my authority was evident in the spiritual realm.

After two weeks I was so adept in the zone that I tapered down to fifteen minutes twice a week. I had built my skill to enter into spiritual warfare and win. This was my preparation for the coming danger.

I thought about how Satan had used my family, other people, the church, and our culture to try to destroy me. I thought about the night of the crisis when he tried to get me to fling myself over the balcony. I thought about the barrage of attacks he accosted me with during the three years afterward. Satan's ultimate plan was to prevent me from being who God created me to be and from doing what God created me to do—a princess waging warfare against Satan. But God is *always* victorious, and He has prepared me to take my position in His army.

> Satan's plan was to prevent me from being who God created me to be—a princess waging warfare against Satan. But God is always victorious!

A catastrophic event is coming. By God's sovereign plan, I will not only survive it, but will cause harm to Satan's kingdom by helping others. In the meantime, God continues to speak truth into my life through His Holy Word, through my prayer time, and through others. I have a deep sense of God's love for me and His desire to be my faithful Father. God delivered me out of my spiritual oppression. I am no longer held captive by demonic influences. I praise God for restoring me back to my Original Design. This is truly freedom in Christ!

Appendix A

Steps to Salvation

ARE YOU A GOOD PERSON? How good do you have to be in order to be good enough to enter into God's holy presence? Romans 3:10 says, "There is none righteous, no, not one." The truth is that our idea of good falls far below God's holy standard and it is impossible for us to meet His criteria on our own. That is why we are all in need of a Savior. Romans 3:23 says, "For all have sinned and fall short of the glory of God." Romans 6:23 tells us, "For the wages of sin is death." Not just physical death, but spiritual death, which is eternal separation from God.

God did not create us to be sinners and become separated from Him. For us to truly love God, He had to create us with a free will. This free will gives us choice, either to love God and serve Him or to disobey God and go our own way. The first man, Adam, chose to disobey God, and he experienced immediate spiritual death. Through Adam's disobedience, sin entered into him, and he reproduced offspring after his new nature as Genesis 5:3 says, "And Adam lived one hundred and thirty years, and begot a son in his own likeness, after his image, and named him Seth." It is through Adam that each and every one of us has a propensity to sin.

Satan is referred to as the "ruler of this world" (John 12:31) and the "god of this world" (2 Cor. 4:4) because to this day he continues to successfully tempt people to sin against God and produce unrighteousness.

God knew that man would sin and fall under Satan's control. He knew we would need a deliverer to release us from our captivity. Before any angel hovered above the throne of glory, before God said, "Let there be light," and most certainly before He declared, "Let us make man in our image," the Triune God appointed the death and resurrection of the eternal Son. First Peter 1:19-20 tells us that Jesus was foreordained before the foundation of the world to redeem us with His blood.

Jesus willingly set aside His deity and "Made Himself of no reputation, taking the form of a bondservant, and coming in the likeness of men. And being found in appearance as a man, He humbled Himself and became obedient to the point of death, even the death of the cross" (Phil. 2:7-8). When Jesus went to the cross, He took our sins upon Himself and in exchange offered us His righteousness. Second Corinthians 5:21 says, "For He made Him who knew no sin to be sin for us, that we might become the righteousness of God in Him."

This passage says we *might* become the righteousness of God in Him. Righteousness, or right standing with God, is not automatically applied to us. Deuteronomy 30:19 says, "I call heaven and earth as witnesses today against you, that I have set before you life and death, blessing and cursing; therefore choose life, that both you and your descendants may live." We have a choice to make and it involves more than just believing with our intellect.

In John 14:6 Jesus said, "I am the way, the truth, and the life. No one comes to the Father except through Me." To receive Jesus's gift of salvation, you must "Confess with your mouth the Lord Jesus and believe in your heart that God has raised Him from the dead, and you will be saved. For with the heart one believes unto righteousness, and with the mouth confession is made unto salvation" (Rom. 10:9-10). When we do this, we are spiritually reborn. When we are born the first time, we have the nature of natural man. When we are "born again," we are partakers of the divine nature (2 Pet. 1:4). As 2 Corinthians 5:17 says, "Therefore, if anyone is in Christ, he is a new creation; old things have passed away; behold, all things have become new."

The first step is that easy. The common misconception that we are saved by being baptized or by doing good works is not true. If it were, Jesus would not have had to die. Ephesians 2:8-9 says, "For by grace you have been saved through faith, and that not of yourselves; it is the gift of God, not of works, lest anyone should boast."

Once we have been saved through faith in Jesus Christ, the second step is to work out our own salvation with fear and trembling (Phil. 2:12). Fear and trembling is not terror of damnation, but a kind of anxiety one has when they feel an important interest is at stake and there is danger of losing it. Working out our salvation is not the same as earning it, which we cannot do.

Jesus shows us how to work out our salvation in Matthew 25:1-12, the parable of the wise and foolish virgins. In this story, Jesus said that the kingdom of Heaven could be likened to ten virgins. Five of them were wise and the other five foolish. The wise ones took oil for their lamps so their lights wouldn't burn out. The foolish ones did not make the extra effort to take oil. The oil was available to all ten, but unlike the lamps, it was not given to them, they had to take it.

When the call came at midnight for the virgins to go into the marriage, only the ones who had taken oil could find their way and enter in. The foolish ones were locked out.

In the same way, salvation (represented by the lamps) is offered to all. But those who are wise will do something with their salvation. We need to be proactive about growing our relationship with God by spending time in prayer and by studying God's Word. These things are the oil that keeps our light burning.

Second Timothy 2:15 says, "Be diligent to present yourself approved to God, a worker who does not need to be ashamed, rightly dividing the word of truth." The word of truth is the Bible and it "is given by inspiration of God, and is profitable for doctrine, for reproof, for correction, for instruction in righteousness (2 Tim. 3:16). In other words, the Bible teaches us who God, Jesus, and the Holy Spirit are and instructs, corrects, and convicts us about what is right and what is required of us in order to lead a life that is pleasing to God.

As we learn about God, we start to see and experience His love, kindness, patience, faithfulness, and goodness. This helps us to love and follow Jesus up the last step to discipleship. This is where we really start to know and serve Jesus, not just know about Him. In Luke 14:27 Jesus said,

> *"And whoever does not bear his cross and come after Me cannot be My disciple. For which of you, intending to build a tower, does not sit down first and count the cost, whether he has enough to finish it— lest, after he has laid the foundation, and is not able to finish, all who see it begin to mock him, saying, 'This man began to build and was not able to finish'? Or what king, going to make war against another king, does not sit down first and consider whether he is able with ten thousand to meet him who*

comes against him with twenty thousand? Or else, while the other is still a great way off, he sends a delegation and asks conditions of peace. So likewise, whoever of you does not forsake all that he has cannot be My disciple."

Bearing our cross can refer to afflictions, trials, or persecutions of one sort or another, but the cross was also an instrument of death. Jesus was saying that He wants us to commit ourselves to Him, even unto death. Being a disciple is hard work and requires sacrifice. It is a call to die to self. It is absolute surrender. If we are not willing to give up our hopes, dreams, and possessions, we are not truly disciples.

The rewards are worth the cost. James 1:12 says, "Blessed is the man who endures temptation; for when he has been approved, he will receive the crown of life which the Lord has promised to those who love Him." And Jesus said, "For whoever desires to save his life will lose it, but whoever loses his life for My sake will find it" (Matt. 16:25). The pleasures and comforts we forego in this life for the sake of Christ will be repaid with endless joys in eternal bliss with God. And during our time on earth, we have the Holy Spirit to help us (John 14:16), teach us (John 14:26), and guide us into all truth (John 16: 13) so that we can be legitimate disciples of Christ. We will think like Jesus, develop His characteristics, and be endued with His power. This is part of God's original design for us.

So, if you believe that Jesus is the Son of God and He died for your sins and you are ready to commit yourself to Him, then you are ready to take the first step.

Pray the following prayer from your heart to become a child of God:

God in Heaven, I admit that I am a sinner and I ask you to forgive me for my sins. I believe in my heart that you sent Jesus, your only begotten Son, to take away my sins by dying on the cross and that you raised Him from the dead.

Jesus, I open my heart and invite you to come in. I ask you to take control of my life and change me into the person you want me to be. I turn my back on evil and I no longer live for myself, but for you Jesus, my Lord and Savior.

HALLELUJAH! You have just been taken out of the kingdom of darkness and put into Jesus's kingdom, the kingdom of light. Luke 15:10 says, "There is joy in the presence of the angels of God over one sinner who repents." A celebration is taking place in Heaven! Godspeed on your new journey!

Appendix B
Baptism in the Holy Spirit

THE HOLY SPIRIT IS THE THIRD PERSON of the Trinity. Like the Father and Son, He has specific roles and functions. A *few* of His activities are to guide us into all truth (John 16:13), lead us (Rom. 8:14), teach us (John 14:26), comfort us (Acts 9:31), empower us (Luke 24:49), glorify and testify of Christ (John 15:26, 16:14), transform us into the image of Christ (2 Cor. 3:18), and distribute spiritual gifts and manifest Himself through the body of Christ (1 Cor. 12:8-11).

Prior to Jesus's death and resurrection, He told His disciples, "And I will pray the Father, and He will give you another Helper, that He may abide with you forever" (John 14:16). The Holy Spirit comes to dwell in us (1 Cor. 3:16) when we accept Jesus Christ as our personal Lord and Savior. In this new birth, we receive a measure of the Holy Spirit, but the Bible tells about an experience subsequent to salvation called baptism, or filling, of the Holy Spirit.

Before Jesus was taken up to heaven, He told His followers they would be empowered as never before. "And being assembled together with them, He commanded them not to depart from Jerusalem, but to wait for the Promise of the Father, "which," He said, "you have heard from Me; for John truly baptized with water, but you shall be baptized with the Holy Spirit not many days from now" (Acts 1:4-5). "But you shall receive power when the Holy Spirit has come upon you; and you shall be witnesses to Me in Jerusalem, and in all Judea and Samaria, and to the end of the earth" (Acts 1: 8).

Acts 2:2-4 tells us what happened to Jesus's disciples when the Holy Spirit came. "And suddenly there came a sound from heaven, as of a rushing mighty wind, and it filled the whole house where they were sitting. Then there appeared to them divided tongues, as of fire, and one sat upon each of them. And they were all filled with the Holy Spirit and began to speak with other tongues, as the Spirit gave them utterance." Speaking in tongues was, and still is, the initial evidence of *believers* receiving the *fullness* of the Holy Spirit.

In Acts 8:14-19 it says, "Now when the apostles who were at Jerusalem heard that Samaria had received the word of God, they sent Peter and John to them, who, when they had come down, prayed for them that they might receive the Holy Spirit. For as yet He had fallen upon none of them. They had only been baptized in the name of the Lord Jesus. Then they laid hands on them, and they received the Holy Spirit. And when Simon saw that through the laying on of the apostles' hands the Holy Spirit was given, he offered them money saying, "Give me this power also, that anyone on whom I lay hands may receive the Holy Spirit." This was not the gift of the Holy Spirit given at salvation, for they already received that when they believed. This was an additional infilling. We can assume they spoke in tongues and perhaps even worked miracles because Simon *saw* something. Only these things would make a sorcerer interested in purchasing Holy Spirit power.

Another example of baptism in the Holy Spirit after conversion is found in Acts chapter nine. This is where Saul, later called Paul, had a personal encounter with Jesus on the way to Damascus. A few days after Saul's experience, God instructed Ananias to go to him. After a short protest, "Ananias went his way and entered the house; and laying his hands on him he said, "Brother Saul, the Lord Jesus, who appeared to you on the road as you came, has sent me that you may receive your sight and be filled with the Holy Spirit" (Acts 9:17). Saul believed in Jesus when he met Him on the road to Damascus. He was considered a "Christian" by Ananias because he referred to him as "brother." Although not directly stated here, we can assume that Saul spoke in other tongues when he was filled with the Spirit, as he later wrote in his letter to the church at Corinth, "I thank my God I speak with tongues more than you all" (1 Cor. 14:18).

Ephesians 5:18 says, "And do not be drunk with wine, in which is dissipation; but be filled with the Spirit." Aside from being a command of God, there are many benefits to being filled with the Holy Spirit.

In 1 Corinthians 14:2, the Apostle Paul wrote, "For he who speaks in a tongue does not speak to men but to God, for no one understands him; however, in the spirit he speaks mysteries." God has given us a supernatural means of directly communicating with Him. Our heavenly language, when used in our personal prayer time, does not need to be understood by us or anyone else to be effective. And when we speak mysteries directly to God, our prayers are encrypted from the devil's ears.

First Corinthians 14:4 says, "He who speaks in a tongue edifies himself…" To edify means to build up. When we pray in tongues our spirit is strengthened, which enables us to be ruled or led by our spirit rather than by our flesh or our mind. When our spirit is strong, we are also more sensitive to the leading of the Holy Spirit. Jude 1:20 speaks about building ourselves up as well. It says, "But you, beloved, building yourselves up on your most holy faith, praying in the Holy Spirit." Praying in the Spirit, or tongues, increases our faith, thus enhancing our relationship with God.

In Romans 8:26-27 it says, "Likewise the Spirit also helps in our weaknesses. For we do not know what we should pray for as we ought, but the Spirit Himself makes intercession for us with groanings which cannot be uttered. Now He who searches the hearts knows what the mind of the Spirit is, because He makes intercession for the saints according to the will of God." When we pray in tongues, it is *our* spirit praying, but the Holy Spirit gives us the utterance. If there is a situation we want to pray about, but we're not sure what God's will is for that circumstance, then we can pray in tongues, being confident we're praying in line with the perfect will of God.

If you want to be baptized in the Holy Spirit, all you have to do is ask. Jesus said, "If a son asks for bread from any father among you, will he give him a stone? Or if he asks for a fish, will he give him a serpent instead of a fish? Or if he asks for an egg, will he offer him a scorpion? If you then, being evil, know how to give good gifts to your children, how much more will your heavenly Father give the Holy Spirit to those who ask Him!" (Luke 11:11-13).

When you ask you must do so in faith, as it's impossible to receive from God without faith. James 1:6-7 says, "But let him ask in faith, with no doubting, for he who doubts is like a wave of the sea driven and tossed by the wind. For let not that man suppose that he will receive anything from the Lord." Furthermore, Jesus said, "Therefore I say to you, whatever things you ask when you pray, believe that you receive them, and you will have them" (Mark 11:24). You first believe and then you will receive what you have asked for (unless you ask amiss; James 4:3).

The most common method used to baptize someone in the Holy Spirit in the early church was the laying on of hands. Peter and John laid their hands on the believers in Samaria and they received the Holy Spirit (Acts 8:17). Ananias used the same technique with Saul (Acts 9:17). Paul repeated the procedure on the disciples at Ephesus (Acts 19:6).

You can have a Spirit-filled believer lay hands on you or you can receive the Holy Spirit by yourself. Either way, after asking in faith, the Holy Spirit will fill you and give you utterance—the ability to speak in tongues. You must yield to the Holy Spirit, as He will not force you to speak and He does not speak for you. You'll need to start moving your lips and tongue to make sounds, even though you'll be speaking out of your spirit. First Corinthians 14:14 says, "For if I pray in a tongue, my spirit prays, but my understanding is unfruitful." Praying in tongues is a spiritual activity that by-passes the intellect.

If you are born-again, desire baptism in the Holy Spirit, and are ready to ask in faith and yield yourself to Him, then say this prayer:

Father, your Word says that you will give the Holy Spirit to those who ask. In the name of Jesus, I ask you in faith to baptize and fill me with your precious Holy Spirit.

By faith I receive the Holy Spirit and the ability to speak in tongues. Holy Spirit, I thank you that you will rise up within me and give me utterance as I exercise my heavenly language.

Now yield to the Holy Spirit and start speaking, not in English, but in your new language! Don't be discouraged if you only speak a few sounds or syllables at first. Much like when you learned English, your vocabulary will expand with time and practice. To stay filled, do it every day!

Appendix C

Authority & Power of God

TO UNDERSTAND OUR AUTHORITY IN CHRIST, we have to start at the beginning. Genesis 1:26 says, "Then God said, 'Let Us make man in Our image, according to Our likeness; let them have dominion over the fish of the sea, over the birds of the air, and over the cattle, over all the earth and over every creeping thing that creeps on the earth.'" God gave humankind dominion, or rule, over the earth and the animal kingdom.

When Adam disobeyed God by eating the fruit, he gave Satan authority in his life. Adam did not hand over his God-given authority of the earth and animals to Satan. And he most certainly did not give Satan authority over other people—only the individual can do that.

With Adam's initial act of disobedience, sin and death came into the world. But Satan did not become the god of this age (2 Cor. 4:4) because Adam yielded to him in the garden one time. Satan has built himself a kingdom on earth because he has successfully deceived most of humankind through the ages to sin against God and therefore follow after him.

God has given us a choice of whose authority we will follow. Romans 6:16 says, "Do you not know that to whom you present yourselves slaves to obey, you are that one's slaves whom you obey, whether of sin *leading* to death, or of obedience *leading* to righteousness?" The one we serve or obey, whether God or Satan, is the one whose authority we come under subjection to. Therefore, Satan only has authority over those who submit to him by sinning or those who let him rule in their lives out of ignorance.

The devil even suggested to Jesus that the kingdoms of the world were handed to him on a silver platter by God. When Jesus was being tempted in the wilderness, the devil took Him up on a high mountain and showed Him all the kingdoms of the world. Satan said to Him, "All this authority I will give You, and their glory; for *this* has been delivered to me, and I give it to whomever I wish" (Luke 4:5-6).

At first glance, this sounds as if Satan has authority over all things. But remember that the devil is a liar. Matthew 28:18 says, "And Jesus came and spoke to them, saying, "All authority has been given to Me in heaven and on earth." God did not designate authority of the world to Satan. God gave all authority to Jesus.

What is this authority that Jesus has? The word *authority* used in the New Testament is the Greek word *exousia*. It is translated into English as delegated influence, power, authority, right, and jurisdiction. When we are submitted to the kingship of Jesus, He gives us the right to use His authority. But the level of spiritual authority we will walk in is directly equal to our degree of submission to God.

What do we need this authority for? Don't we already have rule over the earth and everything on it? Yes. But as Jesus's disciples, we can now use His authority in the spiritual realm against the forces of darkness. Jesus said, "Behold, I give you the authority to trample on serpents and scorpions, and over all the power of the enemy, and nothing shall by any means hurt you" (Luke 10:19).

Exercising God's authority depends in part on our faith. Jesus said, "And these signs will follow those who believe: In My name they will cast out demons; they will speak with new tongues; they will take up serpents; and if they drink anything deadly, it will by no means hurt them; they will lay hands on the sick, and they will recover" (Mark 16:17-18). If we come against the devil and his exploits with weak faith, hoping that maybe our prayers might work, we accomplish nothing except to convince our enemy that we have little or no power against him. We must believe that the Word of God is just as true and powerful for us today as it was for the disciples in Jesus's day.

Jesus not only has authority, but also the power of the Holy Spirit. Luke 4:33-36 gives us an example of this. "Now in the synagogue there was a man who had a spirit of an unclean demon. And he cried out with a loud voice, saying, 'Let *us* alone! What have we to do with You, Jesus of Nazareth? Did You come to destroy us? I know who You are—the Holy One of God!' But Jesus rebuked him, saying, 'Be quiet, and come out of him!' And when the demon had thrown him in *their* midst, it came out of him and did not hurt him. Then they were all amazed and spoke among themselves, saying, 'What a word this *is*! For with authority and power He commands the unclean spirits, and they come out.'"

Authority and power are two distinct attributes. The word for power in regards to the Holy Spirit is the Greek word *dunamis*. It means force, ability, strength, or miraculous power for performing miracles. If Jesus needed both authority and power, then we need both as well. That's why Jesus told his disciples, "Behold, I send the Promise of My Father upon you; but tarry in the city of Jerusalem until you are endued with power from on high" (Luke 24:49). This power was the Holy Spirit.

Now that we understand the authority and power in us, we need to mix that knowledge with our faith and put it into action. Jesus told His disciples, "'And as you go, preach, saying, 'The kingdom of heaven is at hand.' Heal the sick, cleanse the lepers, raise the dead, cast out demons. Freely you have received, freely give" (Matt.10:7-8).

To exercise our God-given authority and release the Holy Spirit power that resides in us, we need to have audacity. According to Merriam-Webster, audacity is the bold disregard of normal restraints, having a fearless daring, or having the will to undertake things that involve risk or danger. Audacious Christians are those who know the source of their authority and power and have the courage and boldness to get in the face of evil spirits and command them to depart.

One final point. Just because we have authority and power over the devil and his works doesn't mean we have a license to run around casting demons out of everyone who is sick or plagued by something. An example of this is in Acts 16:16-18. "Now it happened, as we went to prayer, that a certain slave girl possessed with a spirit of divination met us, who brought her masters much profit by fortune-telling. This girl followed Paul and us, and cried out, saying, 'These men are the servants of the Most High God, who proclaim to us the way of salvation.' And this she did for many days. But Paul, greatly annoyed, turned and said to the spirit, 'I command you in the name of Jesus Christ to come out of her.' And he came out that very hour."

I encourage you to follow Paul's example and wait for the Holy Spirit to give you a word of knowledge, the ability to discern spirits, or unction to act. And when He does, God will be glorified.

Nevertheless do not rejoice in this,
that the spirits are subject to you,
but rather rejoice because
your names are written in heaven.
—Luke 10:20